T0209658

THE
LOST YEARS
OF THE
APOS†LE PAUL

KERRY J. PEACOCK

WESTBOW
PRESS®
A DIVISION OF THOMAS NELSON
& ZONDERVAN

WestBow Press books may be ordered through booksellers or by contacting:

WestBow Press
A Division of Thomas Nelson & Zondervan
1663 Liberty Drive
Bloomington, IN 47403
www.westbowpress.com
844-714-3454

All Scriptures are taken from King James version of the Bible, public domain.

ISBN: 979-8-3850-0130-9 (sc)
ISBN: 979-8-3850-0131-6 (hc)
ISBN: 979-8-3850-0132-3 (e)

Library of Congress Control Number: 2023911553

Print information available on the last page.

WestBow Press rev. date: 08/14/2023

CONTENTS

FOREWORD

Once in a great while, we all experience coming face-to-face with a person whose mission we recognize almost immediately as more dynamic than either we or that person could imagine, much less design and put into motion. Our current way of expressing our appraisal of such is to say, "It's a God thing"—and it is. God uses us to the degree that we allow Him to. When we submit to Him and set out to complete a work that honors Him, He always reveals as much of Himself as He knows we can stand to take in. So it was when Kerry Peacock came to me and announced that he was writing a book seeking to explore the "lost years" of the Apostle Paul, to see and understand more of that great apostle's mind, thought, and passion that "drove him onward." Kerry's stated goals were to see Christ as the Apostle Paul saw Him and to establish the argument that Paul learned about Christ and experienced his "fire in the belly" relationship with Him while in the Arabian Desert during his "lost years."

During that conversation, Kerry briefly sketched out his proposed approach. At the time, I felt as if I needed a road map to follow his plan. However, I recognized that he had done a great deal of thinking, and it was leading him to heights and depths that he had not reached before. He was excited, and it excited me. Then, to challenge me further, he asked me to read his first draft and reflect with him on my reactions to it. I was honored.

When I read a document such as this one, I look for the writer's goals. Then I look at the elements that are presented before judging whether the writer made his case—that is, did he prove his point. In this instance, I found the elements to be presented clearly and, for my part, logically. Then I try to determine if the elements support the goals. Does he make his case? All I can say is that learning what Kerry dug out of Paul's writings is not only impressive, it is inspiring. Yes, he makes his case.

One of the courses in my major in Bible studies from Baylor University was The Life and Writings of the Apostle Paul. It was the first time in my life I had explored those writings in detail. The textbook was arranged chronologically so we did not go from one letter to the next as arranged in the Bible. We instead followed Paul's life chronologically. At the end of the course, when we read about and discussed Paul's death, a sadness settled over me, and I felt as though I had lost a good friend. After I read Kerry's draft, weaving my way through ideas and revelations I had never heard before, I emerged with the realization that I had found my friend Paul again, and he could still teach me and bless me. I was left with a take-away question: have I had my own Arabian Desert experience where I was totally open to what Christ wanted to teach me?

Kerry later told me God wasn't finished yet, that he had more insight. A gift. A gift from God. A gift from Kerry. A gift from God through Kerry to us all. With God's blessing, we are graced with a much-needed book, one that clearly fills a void and is worthy to be used side-by-side with other works of scholarship on the Apostle Paul's life and writings.

Thank you, my friend,
Larry L. Howard

PREFACE

Throughout my life, I have read and been changed by the writings of the Apostle Paul. I have always accepted that his writings were and are the Holy Word of God. I somehow assumed that the moment he was saved, he somehow, automatically, was the fully mature man of God who meets us in the pages of the New Testament. It never occurred to me that he had to learn the ways of Jesus just like we have to learn them—like I have had to learn them.

One day, as I read Romans 7, I began to understand that he had had to struggle. I heard him cry, "Oh wretched man that I am...who can deliver me from this body of death?" For a brief moment, I saw him on his knees before God in the darkness of the desert—the Arabian Desert. I saw his agony. I felt his pain. I knew his struggles. The images were but shadows. I knew I wanted to know this man who has done so much for me and millions of people who have allowed the Holy Spirit to use his words to lead them to a closer walk with our Lord, his Lord, our God, his God.

In this little book, I seek to understand those seemingly lost years of the great apostle. If I could, I would simply like to approach the scriptures to see Paul "through a glass cloudy" (1 Corinthians 13:12) until such time as we shall see each other in heaven's glory "face to face."

Irving Stone wrote a novel about the great artist and sculptor, Michelangelo. It was there that I first became aware of one of the most famous quotations from Michelangelo Buonarroti: "I saw the angel in the marble and carved until I set him free." I am no Michelangelo, but it is my prayer that I might be able to chip away the marble of time and set the great apostle free to step from the shadows into this present light. I want to listen to his words with new understanding. I want to learn of his passion and heart that drove him onward. I want to see Jesus through his eyes. Please Father, show me Paul that I might see more of Jesus Christ!

Many people may be unwilling or unable to set aside their preconceived ideas about Paul. I totally understand. It is difficult to change, particularly one's mind. It is hard to rethink something that we have thought for many years. However, I believe there is something to see that we have not seen. If you can set aside your prejudices (biases) for a few moments and listen with your heart, I believe it will be well worth your efforts. Come with me on the journey to encounter the Saul/Paul of the New Testament.

This book will be divided into two parts. The first focuses on Saul, the chief of sinners, before he was saved, and the second focuses on Paul afterward as the greatest apostle. The contrast between the two is perhaps *the* greatest example of the saving, transforming power of the grace of God through the shed blood of His Son, our Savior, Jesus the Christ.

1

THE MAKING OF THE MAN

To get to the depth of this man named Paul, it is necessary to "know" him if we can. Where did he come from? Who was his family? Where did he live? Who was he within his culture? What was the driving force in his life? Where was he educated? Was he married? Did he have children? Did he know Jesus prior to His resurrection, prior to the Damascus Road experience? All these questions help us understand the man who will spend three years in Arabia being discipled by our Lord Jesus Christ Himself. This is the first step in chipping away the marble that holds and hides the man.

Paul's Pedigree

Let's start with his family. Paul tells us in Acts 22:3 that he was born in Tarsus. According to John Polhill, Jerome, one of history's greatest biblical historians, believed that Paul and his family fled from Judea to Tarsus, but Paul says he was born there.[1] F. F. Bruce, in his book *Paul: Apostle of the Heart Set Free*, gives a wonderful if not somewhat lengthy tracing of the historical setting at the time of Paul's birth. He concludes that Paul's parents were most likely Jews of the dispersion.[2]

Tarsus was a very important city in its day. After Pompey defeated the pirates in 67 BC, the area known as Cilicia became a Roman province with Tarsus as its capital. According to Bruce, Antony and

---

[1]   John B. Polhill, *Paul and His Letters*, (Nashville, TN: B&H Academic, 1999), 36-38

[2]   F.F. Bruce, *Paul: Apostle of the Heart Set Free* (Grand Rapids, MI: Wm. B. Eerdmans Publishing Co., 1977), 42-43

Cleopatra met in Tarsus in 41 BC.[3] Augustus made it possible for the people of Tarsus to become citizens of Rome for 500 drachmae, a coin of the Roman Empire. Also, those who owned property, in my understanding, were granted Roman citizenship. The great city was known for cilicium cloth, which was made of woven goat hair and used in making tents and saddles,[4] according to John Polhill. Tarsus was a city of great institutions of higher learning. Indeed, this city was "no mean city," as mentioned in Acts 21:39. The New International Version translates it as "no ordinary city."

Paul's family, according to his own claim in Acts 22:3, was of the Pharisee sect. That means that he was brought up in a very strict tradition of keeping the law. It also means that he was a man of strict discipline in all things religious. He was trained in the local synagogue. According to Polhill, Paul was very knowledgeable of the Septuagint, the Greek translation of the Old Testament.[5] Paul quoted from it often. Every Jewish father dreamed of sending his son to Jerusalem to finish his education under the finest of Jewish scholars. Perhaps Paul's father already knew of Gamaliel. According to Acts 23:16, Paul had a sister, and she had a son. It is surmised by most scholars that Paul lived with her during his time as a student of Gamaliel.

In the joy-filled book of Philippians, Paul tells us in the third chapter, fifth verse and following, that he was circumcised on the eighth day, which tells us of his parents' strict adherence to the law. He was from the pure stock of Israel, the tribe of Benjamin, a Hebrew of Hebrews (not a Hellenistic Jew), and of course, a Pharisee. He was a man of great zeal as a Jew, and as a Christian, a man of great passion.

Under the watchful eye of his professor/mentor, Gamaliel, the young Saul received the best education a Jewish boy could get from the grandson of the great teacher, Hillel. The picture we need to see of Saul is that of a wealthy young man of privilege and position who sought to be the best at everything he tried to do. There was an air of confident pride about him. He had won and was winning the confidence and respect of

---

[3]   Bruce, 34
[4]   John B. Polhill, *Paul and His Letters*, (Nashville, TN: B&H Academic, 1999),
[5]   John B. Polhill, *Paul and His Letters*, (Nashville, TN: B&H Academic, 1999),

his peer group. He was a rising superstar who was superintelligent and supercommitted. He was Saul of Tarsus.

Paul's Problem

Something happened to affect the rising superstar. He became the chief of sinners (1 Timothy 1:15).

It has occurred to me as I have dared to search for Saul of Tarsus during the three and half years' time of Jesus's ministry that those years are as lost as the years he spent in the desert. If Paul had heard Jesus and seen the things He did, why didn't he say so? There may not be a good answer, but it occurs to me that the Apostle Paul was always careful to shine the spotlight on Jesus. Some of what we are going to consider might have detracted from the work and ministry of the Lord. Perhaps because Jesus's ministry is so fully established in the New Testament, it will be permissible to see Saul of Tarsus in the shadows.

2

SAUL IN THE SHADOWS

On a Christian online forum, a writer called Thrillobyte makes the assertion that "historians agree Paul was in Jerusalem during Jesus's ministry." He draws the conclusion "that means Paul would have been in Jerusalem when Jesus was crucified."[6] The assertion, though I believe it to be correct, would not be accepted by many of the best scholars. Scholars often hang their hats only on the things they can prove. If Paul was in Jerusalem, there is no definitive evidence. However, the possibility of Paul being there opens the door to understanding more about the man, Saul of Tarsus. While it is impossible to prove that Saul was there at the time of Jesus's crucifixion, it is also impossible to prove that he was not.

My first premise that is important to discovering more about Saul of Tarsus during the life and ministry of Jesus is that the gospel of Luke is truly the gospel of Paul. Likewise, it follows that much of what is written in the book of Acts is also influenced heavily by Paul. In an article entitled "Do You Know Which Book in the Bible is Called 'Paul's Gospel'?," Philip Kosloski presents the argument that Paul contributed a great deal to Luke's gospel. Not only was Paul instrumental in the writing of the gospel of Luke but he is also thought to be very much a part of the writing of the Acts of the Apostles.[7]

---

6   Thrillobyte, "Paul Was in Jerusalem during Jesus's Ministry and Crucifixion," City-Data Forum, posted October 31, 2014, www.city-data.com/forum/christianity/2232303-paul-jerusalem-during-jesus-ministry-crucifixion.

7   Philip Kosloski. "Do You Know Which Book in the Bible is Called "Paul's Gospel"?" *Aleteia*, 2019, www.aleteia.org/2019/10/18/do-you-know-which-book-in-the-bible-is-called-pauls-gospel

Luke tells us that he acquired his facts from numerous sources, eyewitnesses, and ministers of the Word. If there was a "Q" source that was used by the gospel writers, I'm certain that Luke was aware of it, though he doesn't mention it directly. The terms "eyewitnesses and ministers of the Word" may well have included Paul (Luke 1:1–4).

Let's look at some of the places where Luke might possibly have an eyewitness account from Paul. I believe that Saul of Tarsus may have been the eyes and ears, not to mention the feet, of the Pharisees and priests. He was sent by these folks to spy on what Jesus was doing and saying and report back to them.

Moreover, Saul may have been involved in the fault-finding efforts. As I will explain later, Saul's turn to the "dark side" came as he approached Jesus as the rich young ruler and was embarrassed by what Jesus said to him. From that experience sprung up a "root of bitterness" (Hebrews 12:14–17), a root that grew in Saul's life, spurring him on to seek the death of Jesus. I have come to believe Paul when he says that he was the "chiefest of sinners."

My journey through the gospel of Luke was like following a trail of breadcrumbs leading to a greater understanding of Saul's role in the story of Jesus. I believe that Saul was simply an interested bystander at first. He just reported to the Sanhedrin what he saw. He began to get closer and closer as it became apparent that Jesus posed a threat to the Jewish religious elite.

I will try to lead us through the gospel of Luke on a treasure hunt to find Saul of Tarsus and better grasp the process of becoming the greatest foe of Jesus. Was Saul always opposed to Jesus? I don't think so. I think at first he was intrigued about what he saw Jesus do and heard Jesus say. When he reported back to the Jewish elders, they probably encouraged him to keep watching, listening, and learning. They, too, were curious about the young rabbi. There were many false messiahs in that day. The Jewish religious leaders were always on guard against another false teacher. These false teachers often stirred up the people against them and against Rome. It often did not end well. Though the Jewish leadership hated the Romans, they were very careful to avoid conflict when possible, so Saul of Tarsus could have been very useful in keeping track of Jesus and His disciples.

My second premise is that Paul was what he claimed to be in 1 Timothy 1:15: "This is a faithful saying and worthy of all acceptation, that Christ Jesus came into the world to save sinners of whom I am chief."

I have always thought that Paul was simply using hyperbole when he made the statement that he was the chief of sinners. In my mind, I was saying, *Oh, Paul. You don't really mean that.* In these last days, I have come to believe that to be true. I can hear you gasp in disbelief and say, "No, no, no! That can't be true of our great hero!"

In my time of study, I have come to believe that Saul of Tarsus became Iago and Darth Vader all wrapped up in one. As the root of bitterness grew in Saul, he became a man obsessed with getting rid of Jesus.

Let me ask you a question. Who knew Judas Iscariot well enough to know his greed and desire to see Jesus proclaim Himself Messiah? I think Saul recognized the same greed in Judas that was in his own heart. It may well have been Saul who, at the request of the Jewish leaders, approached Judas, or perhaps Judas approached Saul. It may have been Saul of Tarsus who put the thirty pieces of silver in Judas's hand. It may well have been Saul of Tarsus who saw Judas throw the thirty pieces of silver on the temple floor. The eyewitness who recorded these events was not Judas. He went out and hanged himself. It was not one of the apostles. They did not have the necessary inside connections. Saul of Tarsus had motive, opportunity, and the will. He demonstrated that will when he held the coats of the men who stoned Stephen.

I believe that Saul of Tarsus was in the crowd crying, "Crucify him! Crucify him!" at the trial of Jesus. He may well have followed in the crowd as they made their way to Golgotha. Saul would have been gratified to see his work being fulfilled in the death of this "false messiah." The root of bitterness was momentarily satiated. Saul stood close to the cross. The evil one, Satan, and his minions threw everything they had at Jesus. Saul of Tarsus was oblivious; his will was being done.

Because he stood so close to the cross on which Jesus was dying, Saul heard much that others did not. In Luke 23:33–43, Luke records the story of the casting of lots for Jesus's clothing. John also records this event. Both John and Saul were close to the cross, but only Saul heard Jesus say, "Father, forgive them for they know not what they do." Perhaps this specifically applies to Saul, as Paul writes in 1 Timothy 1:12–14, "I did it ignorantly in unbelief." John knows more about the seamless coat that had belonged to Jesus. I'm sure that John had admired it many times, but Saul was the one who heard the words of Jesus. John quotes the passage from Psalm 22:18, "They parted my garments among them and upon my vesture did they cast lots." John has paused to watch the soldiers, but Saul has moved to the very foot of the cross. It seems that Saul cannot get enough of Jesus's agony.

William Barclay has long been one of my favorite commentators. In Barclay's commentary on the Gospel of John, he describes the desperate nature of the Jewish leaders, and I would say, of Saul of Tarsus in particular. He recalls how the people, the Jewish leaders in particular, cried out, "We have no King but Caesar!" Barclay calls that statement "the most astonishing *volte-face* in history." Their about face is so total that Pilate must have been awestruck by the anger and bitterness that drove them to madness. "It is a terrible picture," Barclay proclaims.[8] Indeed, it is a terrible picture, and I believe that the madness of this insane crowd was fueled by the bitterness of none other than Saul of Tarsus.

Though it would have made Saul of Tarsus ceremonially unclean to observe the Passover, I believe that he was fully willing to forgo that ritual to see Jesus killed. He would have entered Pilate's palace, a place of potential contamination. He would have been willing to go to Herod's palace (who was perhaps a distant relative) to hear the proceedings, though again risking defilement. Ultimately, he would have been willing most certainly to incur defilement by tracing Jesus's steps to the very foot of the cross. In that moment, the angry bitter heart of Saul of Tarsus had but one thought. Kill him, crucify him—at any cost.

---

8   Barclay, William. *The Gospel of John*, Vol. 2. Philadelphia, PA: The Westminster Press, 1955, 274-276

When a man or woman sells out to bitterness and seeks revenge at all costs, anything and any act of evil is possible. Saul of Tarsus, who had sought truth in his younger days, now sought to kill truth incarnate, Jesus. But even the death of Jesus did not give Saul any peace. The root of bitterness drove him to try to wipe believers in Jesus off the face of the planet.

It is no coincidence that we find Saul holding the coats of the men who stoned Stephen in Acts 7:54–60. I believe that the reason he did not participate in the act itself may have been two-fold. First, the Sanhedrin often, according to sources, would stir up the crowd to violence but keep themselves from the actual deed. Second, Saul was not yet thirty years of age, the age when such things were permissible for a Jewish man. However, some six months later, he was on the road to Damascus, leading the charge to bring judgment into the lives of more Christians. The difference could well be that he had turned thirty. Now he had stepped into the leadership role full bore. He was ready to eradicate those heretics by any means. The root of bitterness had brought forth its malignant flower and fruit.

A poignant question has been asked of me: "Was the Apostle Paul at the crucifixion?" My answer is no, but Saul of Tarsus was. In fact, he had a front row seat. He heard three of the last words of Jesus that no one else records but Luke. Why? Because as a "Pharisee of Pharisees," he was there overseeing from a Jewish perspective the execution of the heretic, rebel, and public enemy number one, Jesus the Christ.

I want to state as clearly as I may that I believe the apostle was the source that Luke used most. If there was a "Q" source used by Mark, Luke, and Matthew, it was never as primary as the Apostle Paul's account to Luke of what he heard and saw.

Many will reject the idea of Saul of Tarsus being there during the ministry of Christ, but I would remind you of something the great apostle himself said in Acts 20:35. He quoted Jesus saying, "It is more blessed to give than receive." Paul says that our Lord Jesus said it, and I believe that.

The problem with this statement is that it is not in any of the gospels. Where did it come from? Inspiration of the Holy Spirit would be one answer. I can accept that, but I find that is not required with the eyewitness accounts that we have. Perhaps our Lord Jesus told him that in the Arabian Desert. That would make sense, but it has the ring to it of a saying well-known in its day. I submit to you that Paul heard it first from the lips of Jesus during Jesus's earthly ministry. For me, this quotation is the "smoking gun" that answers the question about Saul's/Paul's presence during Jesus's earthly ministry.

3

COMPARING GOSPEL ACCOUNTS

As I write this chapter, I realize that not everyone is a scholar, and not everyone wants to read each passage in Luke that is not included in any of the other gospels. If you do not wish to look at each one, simply skip to the next chapter where we pick up the narrative. Please know that the passages in Luke's gospel are important because they display "inside information" that, in my opinion, makes my case that Paul was there during Jesus's ministry. Furthermore, by adding these "inside" views, he proves his intimate familiarity with Jesus and His disciples.

Also, let me make this confession: I think in King James. That is, I always quote from the King James Version. I do *not* mean to imply that the King James Version is the only version, though it is for some. I encourage you to use the translation that you prefer as you research what is said in any of the Bible passages quoted, and especially these passages found only in Luke's gospel.

In so many places in the gospels, it is apparent that the source retelling the events is watching from a close, but not immediate, point of view. While it is impossible to point to any one passage and say it is definitely the Apostle Paul's recollection, looking at all the passages together, it is almost impossible to deny the apostle's influence. I am including many of such passages that I was able to isolate using A. T. Robertson's *Harmony of the Gospels*. These passages appear in Luke's gospel and no other. Many are from the Pharisee's point of view.

> Forasmuch as many have taken in hand to set forth in order a declaration of those things which are most surely believed among us, Even as they delivered them unto us, which from the beginning were eyewitnesses,

and ministers of the word; It seemed good to me also, having had perfect understanding of all things from the very first, to write unto thee in order, most excellent Theophilus, That thou mightest know the certainty of those things, wherein thou hast been instructed. (Luke 1:1–4 KJV)

Robertson begins by reiterating what Luke says, that he received his information from eyewitnesses. This could have included Saul of Tarsus.

But when he saw many of the Pharisees and Sadducees come to his baptism, he said unto them, "O generation of vipers, who hath warned you to flee from the wrath to come? Bring forth therefore fruits meet for repentance: And think not to say within yourselves, 'We have Abraham to our father': for I say unto you, that God is able of these stones to raise up children unto Abraham. And now also the axe is laid unto the root of the trees: therefore every tree which bringeth not forth good fruit is hewn down, and cast into the fire." (Matthew 3:7–10 KJV)

This passage tells that the Pharisees and Sadducees came out to hear John the Baptist. Was Saul possibly in this group?

Now when all the people were baptized, it came to pass, that Jesus also being baptized, and praying, the heaven was opened, And the Holy Ghost descended in a bodily shape like a dove upon him, and a voice came from heaven, which said, Thou art my beloved Son; in thee I am well pleased. And Jesus himself began to be about thirty years of age, being (as was supposed) the son of Joseph, which was the son of Heli. (Luke 3:21–23 KJV)

This is the account of Jesus's baptism recorded in Luke. Was Saul there?

And this is the record of John, when the Jews sent priests and Levites from Jerusalem to ask him, Who art thou? And he confessed, and denied not; but confessed, I am not the Christ. And they asked him, What then? Art thou Elias? And he saith, I am not. Art thou that prophet? And he answered, No. Then said they unto him, Who art thou? that we may give an answer to them that sent us. What sayest thou of thyself? He said, I am the voice of one crying in the wilderness, Make straight the way of the Lord, as said the prophet Esaias. And they which were sent were of the Pharisees. And they asked him, and said unto him, Why baptizest thou then, if thou be not that Christ, nor Elias, neither that prophet? John answered them, saying, I baptize with water: but there standeth one among you, whom ye know not; He it is, who coming after me is preferred before me, whose shoe's latchet I am not worthy to unloose. These things were done in Bethabara beyond Jordan, where John was baptizing. (John 1:19–28 KJV)

Not only were the Pharisees concerned about Jesus, they were also concerned about John the Baptist. The committee of members of the Sanhedrin, of which Saul was a member, came to John the Baptist to impugn who he was. Was Saul in this group?

Jesus then came down to Capernaum, a city of Galilee, and taught them on the sabbath days. And they were astonished at his doctrine: for his word was with power. And in the synagogue, there was a man, which had a spirit of an unclean devil, and cried out with a loud voice, Saying, Let us alone; what have we to do with thee, thou Jesus of Nazareth? art thou come to destroy us? I know thee who thou art; the Holy One of God. And Jesus rebuked him, saying, Hold thy peace, and come out of him. And when the devil had thrown him in the midst, he came out of him, and hurt him not. And they were all amazed, and spake among themselves, saying, What a word is this! for with authority and power he commandeth the unclean spirits, and they come out. And the fame of him went out into every place of the country round about. (Luke 4:31–37 KJV)

Saul could have seen the man with a demon delivered. This would have caused quite a stir among Saul's peers.

And he arose out of the synagogue, and entered into Simon's house. And Simon's wife's mother was taken with a great fever; and they besought him for her. And he stood over her, and rebuked the fever; and it left her: and immediately she arose and ministered unto them. Now when the sun was setting, all they that had any sick with divers diseases brought them unto him; and he laid his hands on every one of them, and healed them. And devils also came out of many, crying out, and saying, Thou art Christ the Son of God. And he rebuking them suffered them not to speak: for they knew that he was Christ. (Luke 4:38–41 KJV)

Was Saul at the healing of Simon Peter's mother-in-law? He could have heard the devils testify of Jesus as the Son of God.

And it came to pass on a certain day, as he was teaching, that there were Pharisees and doctors of the law sitting by, which were come out of every town of Galilee, and Judaea, and Jerusalem: and the power of the Lord was present to heal them. And, behold, men brought in a bed a man which was taken with a palsy: and they sought means to bring him in, and to lay him before him. And when they could not find by what way they might bring him in because of the multitude, they went upon the housetop, and let him down through the tiling with his couch into the midst before Jesus. And when he saw their faith, he said unto him, Man, thy sins are forgiven thee. And the scribes and the Pharisees began to reason, saying, Who is this which speaketh blasphemies? Who can forgive sins, but God alone? But when Jesus perceived their thoughts, he answering said unto them, What reason ye in your hearts? Whether is easier, to say, Thy sins be forgiven thee; or to say, Rise up and walk? But that ye may know that the Son of man hath power upon earth to forgive sins, (he said unto the sick of the palsy,) I say unto thee, Arise, and take up thy couch, and go into thine house. And immediately he rose up before them, and took up that whereon he lay, and departed to his own house, glorifying God. And they were all amazed, and they glorified God, and were filled with fear, saying, We have seen strange things to day. (Luke 5:17–26 KJV)

Perhaps Saul was in the house when the four brought their friend and let him down through the roof. From his lips may have come, "Who is this that speaketh blasphemy? Who can forgive sins but God himself?" Saul would have known what they were thinking.

And after these things he went forth, and saw a publican, named Levi, sitting at the receipt of custom: and he said unto him, Follow me. And he left all, rose up, and followed him. And Levi made him a great feast in his own house: and there was a great company of publicans and of others that sat down with them. But their scribes and Pharisees murmured against his disciples, saying, Why do ye eat and drink with publicans and sinners? And Jesus answering said unto them, They that are whole need not a physician; but they that are sick. I came not to call the righteous, but sinners to repentance. (Luke 5:27–32 KJV)

Saul may have questioned why Jesus was eating with publicans and sinners. His training would have made him repulsed by such a thing.

> And it came to pass on the second sabbath after the first, that he went through the corn fields; and his disciples plucked the ears of corn, and did eat, rubbing them in their hands. And certain of the Pharisees said unto them, Why do ye that which is not lawful to do on the sabbath days? And Jesus answering them said, Have ye not read so much as this, what David did, when himself was an hungred, and they which were with him; How he went into the house of God, and did take and eat the shewbread, and gave also to them that were with him; which it is not lawful to eat but for the priests alone? And he said unto them, That the Son of man is Lord also of the sabbath. (Luke 6:1–5 KJV)

Saul may have been among the Pharisees who accused Jesus's disciples of breaking Sabbath laws because they picked corn and ate it.

> And it came to pass also on another sabbath, that he entered into the synagogue and taught: and there was a man whose right hand was withered. And the scribes and Pharisees watched him, whether he would heal on the sabbath day; that they might find an accusation against him. But he knew their thoughts, and said to the man which had the withered hand, Rise up, and stand forth in the midst. And he arose and stood forth. Then said Jesus unto them, I will ask you one thing; Is it lawful on the sabbath days to do good, or to do evil? to save life, or to destroy it? And looking round about upon them all, he said unto the man, Stretch forth thy hand. And he did so: and his hand was restored whole as the other. And they were filled with madness; and communed one with another what they might do to Jesus. (Luke 6:6–11 KJV)

Saul may have been one of the ones who was "filled with madness."

> And he lifted up his eyes on his disciples, and said, Blessed be ye poor: for yours is the kingdom of God. Blessed are ye that hunger now: for ye shall be filled. Blessed are ye that weep now: for ye shall laugh. Blessed are ye, when men shall hate you, and when they shall separate you from their company, and shall reproach you, and cast out your name as evil, for the Son of man's sake. Rejoice ye in that day, and leap for joy: for, behold, your reward is great in heaven: for in the like manner did their fathers unto the prophets. But woe unto you that are rich! for ye have received your consolation. Woe unto you that are full! for ye shall hunger. Woe unto you that laugh now! for ye shall mourn and weep. Woe unto you, when all men shall speak well of you! for so did their fathers to the false prophets. (Luke 6:20–26 KJV)

Luke's retelling of the Sermon on the Mount focuses on different things than Matthew's account. Luke includes the statement, "But woe unto you that are rich! For ye have received your consolation." Luke records what perhaps struck Saul most. It was the same old battle with covetousness and greed.

> Judge not, and ye shall not be judged: condemn not, and ye shall not be condemned: forgive, and ye shall be forgiven: Give, and it shall be given unto you; good measure, pressed down, and shaken together, and running over, shall men give into your bosom. For with the same measure that ye mete withal it shall be measured to you again. And he spake a parable unto them, Can the blind lead the blind? shall they not both fall into the ditch? The disciple is not above his master: but every one that is perfect shall be as his master. And why beholdest thou the mote that is in

thy brother's eye, but perceivest not the beam that is in thine own eye? Either how canst thou say to thy brother, Brother, let me pull out the mote that is in thine eye, when thou thyself beholdest not the beam that is in thine own eye? Thou hypocrite, cast out first the beam out of thine own eye, and then shalt thou see clearly to pull out the mote that is in thy brother's eye. (Luke 6:37–42 KJV)

Luke includes more material than Matthew, and it would have been things that had particularly caught the attention of Saul. Luke writes, "It shall be given unto you; good measure, pressed down, shaken together, running over, shall be given into your bosom." Again, we see the desire for wealth.

And it came to pass the day after, that he went into a city called Nain; and many of his disciples went with him, and much people. Now when he came nigh to the gate of the city, behold, there was a dead man carried out, the only son of his mother, and she was a widow: and much people of the city was with her. And when the Lord saw her, he had compassion on her, and said unto her, Weep not. And he came and touched the bier: and they that bare him stood still. And he said, Young man, I say unto thee, Arise. And he that was dead sat up, and began to speak. And he delivered him to his mother. And there came a fear on all: and they glorified God, saying, That a great prophet is risen up among us; and, That God hath visited his people. And this rumour of him went forth throughout all Judaea, and throughout all the region round about. (Luke 7:11–17 KJV)

This passage, a story not found in the other gospels, pays particular attention to "there came a fear on all, and they glorified God saying that a great prophet is risen among us." Though he doubted, Saul was impressed.

And all the people that heard him, and the publicans, justified God, being baptized with the baptism of John. But the Pharisees and lawyers rejected the counsel of God against themselves, being not baptized of him. (Luke 7:29–30 KJV)

Luke adds that "the Pharisees and lawyers rejected the counsel of God being not baptized of him." The tide was turning from curiosity to concern.

And one of the Pharisees desired him that he would eat with him. And he went into the Pharisee's house, and sat down to meat. And, behold, a woman in the city, which was a sinner, when she knew that Jesus sat at meat in the Pharisee's house, brought an alabaster box of ointment, And stood at his feet behind him weeping, and began to wash his feet with tears, and did wipe them with the hairs of her head, and kissed his feet, and anointed them with the ointment. Now when the Pharisee which had bidden him saw it, he spake within himself, saying, This man, if he were a prophet, would have known who and what manner of woman this is that toucheth him: for she is a sinner. And Jesus answering said unto him, Simon, I have somewhat to say unto thee. And he saith, Master, say on. There was a certain creditor which had two debtors: the one owed five hundred pence, and the other fifty. And when they had nothing to pay, he frankly forgave them both. Tell me therefore, which of them will love him most? Simon answered and said, I suppose that he, to whom he forgave most. And he said unto him, Thou hast rightly judged. And he turned to the woman, and said unto Simon, Seest thou this woman? I entered into thine house, thou gavest me no water for my feet: but she hath washed my feet with tears, and wiped them with the hairs of her head. Thou gavest me no kiss: but this woman since the time I came in hath not ceased to kiss my feet. My head with oil thou didst not anoint: but this woman hath anointed my feet with ointment. Wherefore I say unto thee, Her sins, which are many, are forgiven; for she loved much: but to whom little is forgiven, the same loveth little. And he said unto her, Thy sins are forgiven. And they that sat at meat with him began to say within themselves, Who is this that forgiveth sins also? And he said to the woman, Thy faith hath saved thee; go in peace. (Luke 7:36–50 KJV)

Luke, and Luke alone, records the story of the meal at Simon the Pharisee's house. Surely Saul was there with his fellow Pharisees.

And, behold, there came a man named Jairus, and he was a ruler of the synagogue: and he fell down at Jesus's feet, and besought him that he would come into his house. (Luke 8:41 KJV)

Only Luke tells us the name of the ruler of the synagogue, Jairus. Saul would more than likely have known him and his name.

But the ship was now in the midst of the sea, tossed with waves: for the wind was contrary. And in the fourth watch of the night Jesus went unto them, walking on the sea. And when the disciples saw him walking on the sea, they were troubled, saying, It is a spirit; and they cried out for fear. But straightway Jesus spake unto them, saying, Be of good cheer; it is I; be not afraid. And Peter answered him and said, Lord, if it be thou, bid me come unto thee on the water. And he said, Come. And when Peter was come down out of the ship, he walked on the water, to go to Jesus. But when he saw the wind boisterous, he was afraid; and beginning to sink, he cried, saying, Lord, save me. And immediately Jesus stretched forth his hand, and caught him, and said unto him, O thou of little faith, wherefore didst thou doubt? And when they were come into the ship, the wind ceased. Then they that were in the ship came and worshipped him, saying, Of a truth thou art the Son of God. (Matthew 14:24–33 KJV)

Luke is silent about the peril of the disciples in the boat and Peter walking on the water. Luke's source, Saul, was elsewhere.

The day following, when the people which stood on the other side of the sea saw that there was none other boat there, save that one whereinto his disciples were entered, and that Jesus went not with his disciples into the boat, but that his disciples were gone away alone; (Howbeit there came other boats from Tiberias nigh unto the place where they did eat bread, after that the Lord had given thanks:) When the people therefore saw that Jesus was not there, neither his disciples, they also took shipping, and came to Capernaum, seeking for Jesus. And when they had found him on the other side of the sea, they said unto him, Rabbi, when camest thou hither? Jesus answered them and said, Verily, verily, I say unto you, Ye seek me, not because ye saw the miracles, but because ye did eat of the loaves, and were filled. Labour not for the meat which perisheth, but for that meat which endureth unto everlasting life, which the Son of man shall give unto you: for him hath God the Father sealed. Then said they unto him, What shall we do, that we might work the works of God? Jesus answered and said unto them, This is the work of God, that ye believe on him whom he hath sent. They said therefore unto him, What sign shewest thou then, that we may see, and believe thee? what dost thou work? Our fathers did eat manna in the desert; as it is written, He gave them bread from heaven to eat. Then Jesus said unto them, Verily, verily, I say unto you, Moses gave you not that bread from heaven; but my Father giveth you the true bread from heaven. For the bread of God is he which cometh down from heaven, and giveth life unto the world. Then said they unto him, Lord, evermore give us this bread. And Jesus said unto them, I am the bread of life: he that cometh to me shall never hunger; and he that believeth on me shall never thirst. But I said unto you, That ye also have seen me, and believe not. All that the Father giveth me shall come to me; and him that cometh to me I will in no wise cast out. For I came down from heaven, not to do mine own will, but the will of him that sent me. And this is the Father's will which hath sent me, that of all which he hath given me I should lose nothing, but should raise it up again at the last day. And this is the will of him that sent me, that every one which seeth the Son, and believeth on him, may have everlasting life: and I will raise him up at the last day. The Jews then murmured at him, because he said, I am the bread which came down from heaven. And they said, Is not this Jesus, the son of Joseph, whose father and mother we know? how is it then that he saith, I came down from heaven? Jesus therefore answered and said unto them, Murmur not among yourselves. No man can come to me, except the Father which hath sent me draw him: and I will raise him up at the last day. It is written in the prophets, And they shall be all taught of God. Every man therefore that hath heard, and hath learned of the Father, cometh unto me. Not that any man hath seen the Father, save he which is of God, he hath seen the Father. Verily, verily, I say unto you, He that believeth on me hath everlasting life. I am that bread of life. Your fathers did eat manna in the wilderness, and are dead. This is the bread which cometh down from heaven, that a man may eat thereof, and not die. I am the living bread which came down from heaven: if any man eat of this bread, he shall live for ever: and the bread that I will give is my flesh, which I will give for the life of the world. The Jews therefore strove among themselves, saying, How can this man give us his flesh to eat? Then Jesus said unto them, Verily, verily, I say unto you, Except ye eat the flesh of the Son of man, and drink his blood, ye have no life in you. Whoso eateth my flesh, and drinketh my blood, hath eternal life; and I will raise him up at the last day. For my flesh is meat indeed, and my blood is drink indeed. He that eateth my flesh, and drinketh my blood, dwelleth in me, and I in him. As the living Father hath sent me, and I live by the Father: so he that eateth me, even he shall live by me. This is that bread which came down from heaven: not as your fathers did eat manna, and are dead: he that eateth of this bread shall live for ever. These things said he in the synagogue, as he taught in Capernaum. Many therefore of his disciples, when they had heard this, said, This is an hard saying; who can hear it? When Jesus knew in himself that his disciples murmured at it, he said unto them, Doth this offend you? What and if ye shall see the Son of man ascend up where he was before? It is the spirit that quickeneth; the flesh profiteth nothing: the words that I speak unto you, they are spirit, and they are life. But there are some of you that believe not. For Jesus knew from the beginning who they were that believed not, and who should betray him. And he said, Therefore said I unto you, that no man can come unto me, except it were given unto him of my Father. From that time many of his disciples went back, and walked no more with him. Then said Jesus unto the twelve, Will ye also go away? Then Simon Peter answered him, Lord, to whom shall we go? thou hast the words of eternal life. And we believe and are sure that thou art that Christ, the Son of the living God. Jesus answered them, Have not I chosen you twelve, and one of you is a devil? He spake of Judas Iscariot the son of Simon: for he it was that should betray him, being one of the twelve. (John 6:22–71 KJV)

This recounts the collapse of the Galilean campaign because Jesus would not conform to popular messianic expectations. Jesus encouraged His disciples. Luke was silent. Saul, obviously, was not there.

And when his disciples were come to the other side, they had forgotten to take bread. Then Jesus said unto them, Take heed and beware of the leaven of the Pharisees and of the Sadducees. And they reasoned among themselves, saying, It is because we have taken no bread. Which when Jesus perceived, he said unto them, O ye of little faith, why reason ye among yourselves, because ye have brought no bread? Do ye not yet understand, neither remember the five loaves of the five thousand, and how many baskets ye took up? Neither the seven loaves of the four thousand, and how many baskets ye took up? How is it that ye do not understand that I spake it not to you concerning bread, that ye should beware of the leaven of the Pharisees and of the Sadducees? Then understood they how that he bade them not beware of the leaven of bread, but of the doctrine of the Pharisees and of the Sadducees. (Matthew 16:5–12 KJV)

Much is said in this passage that would not have been known by anyone but the twelve. Luke is silent.

And as Jesus passed by, he saw a man which was blind from his birth. And his disciples asked him, saying, Master, who did sin, this man, or his parents, that he was born blind? Jesus answered, Neither hath this man sinned, nor his parents: but that the works of God should be made manifest in him. I must work the works of him that sent me, while it is day: the night cometh, when no man can work. As long as I am in the world, I am the light of the world. When he had thus spoken, he spat on the ground, and made clay of the spittle, and he anointed the eyes of the blind man with the clay, And said unto him, Go, wash in the pool of Siloam, (which is by interpretation, Sent.) He went his way therefore, and washed, and came seeing. The neighbours therefore, and they which before had seen him that he was blind, said, Is not this he that sat and begged? Some said, This is he: others said, He is like him: but he said, I am he. Therefore said they unto him, How were thine eyes opened? He answered and said, A man that is called Jesus made clay, and anointed mine eyes, and said unto me, Go to the pool of Siloam, and wash: and I went and washed, and I received sight. Then said they unto him, Where is he? He said, I know not. They brought to the Pharisees him that aforetime was blind. And it was the sabbath day when Jesus made the clay, and opened his eyes. Then again the Pharisees also asked him how he had received his sight. He said unto them, He put clay upon mine eyes, and I washed, and do see. Therefore said some of the Pharisees, This man is not of God, because he keepeth not the sabbath day. Others said, How can a man that is a sinner do such miracles? And there was a division among them. They say unto the blind man again, What sayest thou of him, that he hath opened thine eyes? He said, He is a prophet. But the Jews did not believe concerning him, that he had been blind, and received his sight, until they called the parents of him that had received his sight. And they asked them, saying, Is this your son, who ye say was born blind? how then doth he now see? His parents answered them and said, We know that this is our son, and that he was born blind: But by what means he now seeth, we know not; or who hath opened his eyes, we know not: he is of age; ask him: he shall speak for himself. These words spake his parents, because they feared the Jews: for the Jews had agreed already, that if any man did confess that he was Christ, he should be put out of the synagogue. Therefore said his parents, He is of age; ask him. Then again called they the man that was blind, and said unto him, Give God the praise: we know that this man is a sinner. He answered and said, Whether he be a sinner or no, I know not: one thing I know, that, whereas I was blind, now I see. Then said they to him again, What did he to thee? how opened he thine eyes? He answered them, I have told you already, and ye did not hear: wherefore would ye hear it again? will ye also be his disciples? Then they reviled him, and said, Thou art his disciple; but we are Moses' disciples. We know that God spake unto Moses: as for this fellow, we know not from whence he is. The man answered and said unto them, Why herein is a marvellous thing, that ye know not from whence he is, and yet he hath opened mine eyes. Now we know that God heareth not sinners: but if any man be a worshipper of God, and doeth his will, him he heareth. Since the world began was it not heard that any man opened the eyes of one that was born blind. If this man were not of God, he could do nothing. They answered and said unto him, Thou wast altogether born in sins, and dost thou teach us? And they cast him out. Jesus heard that they had cast him out; and when he had found him, he said unto him, Dost thou believe on the Son of God? He answered and said, Who is he, Lord, that I might believe on him? And Jesus said unto him, Thou hast both seen him, and it is he that talketh with thee. And he said, Lord, I believe. And he worshipped him. And Jesus said, For judgment I am come into this world, that they which see not might see; and that they which see might be made blind. And some of the Pharisees which were with him heard these words, and said unto him, Are we blind also? Jesus said unto them, If ye were blind, ye should have no sin: but now ye say, We see; therefore your sin remaineth. (John 9:1–41 KJV)

Luke neither comments on nor records the story of the healing of the man born blind. I am not sure why Luke does not share this story. Perhaps Paul felt that John had covered the story adequately. The story shows the mindset and attitude of the Pharisees and their rising anger.

Verily, verily, I say unto you, He that entereth not by the door into the sheepfold, but climbeth up some other way, the same is a thief and a robber. But he that entereth in by the door is the shepherd of the sheep. To him the porter openeth; and the sheep hear his voice: and he calleth his own sheep by name, and leadeth them out. And when he putteth forth his own sheep, he goeth before them, and the sheep follow him: for they know his voice. And a stranger will they not follow, but will flee from him: for they know not the voice of strangers. This parable spake Jesus unto them: but they understood not what things they were which he spake unto them. Then said Jesus unto them again, Verily, verily, I say unto you, I am the door of the sheep. All that ever came before me are thieves and robbers: but the sheep did not hear them. I am the door: by me if any man enter in, he shall be saved, and shall go in and out, and find pasture. The thief cometh not, but for to steal, and to kill, and to destroy: I am come that they might have life, and that they might have it more abundantly. I am the good shepherd: the good shepherd giveth his life for the sheep. But he that is an hireling, and not the shepherd, whose own the sheep are not, seeth the wolf coming, and leaveth the sheep, and fleeth: and the wolf catcheth them, and scattereth the sheep. The hireling fleeth, because he is an hireling, and careth not for the sheep. I am the good shepherd, and know my sheep, and am known of mine. As the

Father knoweth me, even so know I the Father: and I lay down my life for the sheep. And other sheep I have, which are not of this fold: them also I must bring, and they shall hear my voice; and there shall be one fold, and one shepherd. Therefore doth my Father love me, because I lay down my life, that I might take it again. No man taketh it from me, but I lay it down of myself. I have power to lay it down, and I have power to take it again. This commandment have I received of my Father. There was a division therefore again among the Jews for these sayings. And many of them said, He hath a devil, and is mad; why hear ye him? Others said, These are not the words of him that hath a devil. Can a devil open the eyes of the blind? (John 10:1–21 KJV)

As Jesus taught the crowds, the Jewish leaders were there: scribes, Sadducees, and Pharisees. There was a division in their opinion. Many thought he had a devil and was mad; many couldn't believe that a devil would heal a blind man. I think Saul was leaning further and further toward the first group.

And, behold, a certain lawyer stood up, and tempted him, saying, Master, what shall I do to inherit eternal life? He said unto him, What is written in the law? how readest thou? And he answering said, Thou shalt love the Lord thy God with all thy heart, and with all thy soul, and with all thy strength, and with all thy mind; and thy neighbour as thyself. (Luke 10:25–27 KJV)

The lawyer's question is recorded by Luke. Again, this is something Saul would know about and may have been there to hear.

And as he spake, a certain Pharisee besought him to dine with him: and he went in, and sat down to meat. And when the Pharisee saw it, he marvelled that he had not first washed before dinner. And the Lord said unto him, Now do ye Pharisees make clean the outside of the cup and the platter; but your inward part is full of ravening and wickedness. Ye fools, did not he that made that which is without make that which is within also? But rather give alms of such things as ye have; and, behold, all things are clean unto you. But woe unto you, Pharisees! for ye tithe mint and rue and all manner of herbs, and pass over judgment and the love of God: these ought ye to have done, and not to leave the other undone. Woe unto you, Pharisees! for ye love the uppermost seats in the synagogues, and greetings in the markets. Woe unto you, scribes and Pharisees, hypocrites! for ye are as graves which appear not, and the men that walk over them are not aware of them. Then answered one of the lawyers, and said unto him, Master, thus saying thou reproachest us also. And he said, Woe unto you also, ye lawyers! for ye lade men with burdens grievous to be borne, and ye yourselves touch not the burdens with one of your fingers. Woe unto you! for ye build the sepulchres of the prophets, and your fathers killed them. Truly ye bear witness that ye allow the deeds of your fathers: for they indeed killed them, and ye build their sepulchres. Therefore also said the wisdom of God, I will send them prophets and apostles, and some of them they shall slay and persecute: That the blood of all the prophets, which was shed from the foundation of the world, may be required of this generation; From the blood of Abel unto the blood of Zacharias which perished between the altar and the temple: verily I say unto you, It shall be required of this generation. Woe unto you, lawyers! for ye have taken away the key of knowledge: ye entered not in yourselves, and them that were entering in ye hindered. And as he said these things unto them, the scribes and the Pharisees began to urge him vehemently, and to provoke him to speak of many things: Laying wait for him, and seeking to catch something out of his mouth, that they might accuse him. (Luke 11:37–54 KJV)

Luke, and Luke alone, records this story of Jesus being invited to the Pharisee's house for lunch. Jesus takes the Pharisees to task. Surely every word stung the young Saul.

Luke Chapters 12 and 13

A number of stories in these chapters are not in the other gospels, and are things that Saul may have heard and observed firsthand.

The same day there came certain of the Pharisees, saying unto him, Get thee out, and depart hence: for Herod will kill thee. And he said unto them, Go ye, and tell that fox, Behold, I cast out devils, and I do cures today and tomorrow, and the third day I shall be perfected. (Luke 13:31–32 KJV)

This is a curious story related only by Luke. Some of the Pharisees warned Jesus that Herod was trying to kill him. Saul would likely have known, and maybe even gave them the news.

Luke 14:1 through Luke 17:10

These passages contain stories of continuing dialog with Pharisees, very important to Saul of Tarsus.

Luke 17:11 through Luke 18:14

This is a very interesting record of Jesus speaking a parable to "certain which trusted in themselves that they were righteous, and despised others" (Luke 18:9 KJV). I think Jesus may have spoken directly to Saul here.

And a certain ruler asked him, saying, Good Master, what shall I do to inherit eternal life? And Jesus said unto him, Why callest thou me good? none is good, save one, that is, God. Thou knowest the commandments, Do not commit adultery, Do not kill, Do not steal, Do not bear false witness, Honour thy father and thy mother. And he said, All these have I kept from my youth up. Now when Jesus heard these things, he said unto him, Yet lackest thou one thing: sell all that thou hast, and distribute unto the poor, and thou shalt have treasure in heaven: and come, follow me. And when he heard this, he was very sorrowful: for he was very rich. And when Jesus saw that he was very sorrowful, he said, How hardly shall they that have riches enter into the kingdom of God! For it is easier for a camel to go through a needle's eye, than for a rich man to enter into the kingdom of God. And they that heard it said, Who then can be saved? And he said, The things which are impossible with men are possible with God. Then Peter said, Lo, we have left all, and followed thee. And he said unto them, Verily I say unto you, There is no man that hath left house, or parents, or brethren, or wife, or children, for the kingdom of God's sake, Who shall not receive manifold more in this present time, and in the world to come life everlasting. (Luke 18:18–30 KJV)

Matthew, Mark, and Luke all record the story of the rich, young ruler. It is truly a key story if all record it.

After this, the tenor of the account changes to show much greater animosity.

And Jesus entered and passed through Jericho. And, behold, there was a man named Zacchaeus, which was the chief among the publicans, and he was rich. And he sought to see Jesus who he was; and could not for the press, because he was little of stature. And he ran before, and climbed up into a sycamore tree to see him: for he was to pass that way. And when Jesus came to the place, he looked up, and saw him, and said unto him, Zacchaeus, make haste, and come down; for today I must abide at thy house. And he made haste, and came down, and received him joyfully. And when they saw it, they all murmured, saying, That he was gone to be guest with a man that is a sinner. And Zacchaeus stood, and said unto the Lord: Behold, Lord, the half of my goods I give to the poor; and if I have taken any thing from any man by false accusation, I restore him fourfold. And Jesus said unto him, This day is salvation come to this house, forsomuch as he also is a son of Abraham. For the Son of man is come to seek and to save that which was lost. And as they heard these things, he added and spake a parable, because he was nigh to Jerusalem, and because they thought that the kingdom of God should immediately appear. He said therefore, A certain nobleman went into a far country to receive for himself a kingdom, and to return. And he called his ten servants, and delivered them ten pounds, and said unto them, Occupy till I come. But his citizens hated him, and sent a message after him, saying, We will not have this man to reign over us. And it came to pass, that when he was returned, having received the kingdom, then he commanded these servants to be called unto him, to whom he had given the money, that he might know how much every man had gained by trading. Then came the first, saying, Lord, thy pound hath gained ten pounds. And he said unto him, Well, thou good servant: because thou hast been faithful in a very little, have thou authority over ten cities. And the second came, saying, Lord, thy pound hath gained five pounds. And he said likewise to him, Be thou also over five cities. And another came, saying, Lord, behold, here is thy pound, which I have kept laid up in a napkin: For I feared thee, because thou art an austere man: thou takest up that thou layedst not down, and reapest that thou didst not sow. And he saith unto him, Out of thine own mouth will I judge thee, thou wicked servant. Thou knewest that I was an austere man, taking up that I laid not down, and reaping that I did not sow: Wherefore then gavest not thou my money into the bank, that at my coming I might have required mine own with usury?

And he said unto them that stood by, Take from him the pound, and give it to him that hath ten pounds. (And they said unto him, Lord, he hath ten pounds.) For I say unto you, That unto every one which hath shall be given; and from him that hath not, even that he hath shall be taken away from him. But those mine enemies, which would not that I should reign over them, bring hither, and slay them before me. And when he had thus spoken, he went before, ascending up to Jerusalem. (Luke 19:1–28 KJV)

Once again, the story is about a chief publican, someone whom Saul may well have known.

And it came to pass, when he was come nigh to Bethphage and Bethany, at the mount called the mount of Olives, he sent two of his disciples, Saying, Go ye into the village over against you; in the which at your entering ye shall find a colt tied, whereon yet never man sat: loose him, and bring him hither. And if any man ask you, Why do ye loose him? thus shall ye say unto him, Because the Lord hath need of him. And they that were sent went their way, and found even as he had said unto them. And as they were loosing the colt, the owners thereof said unto them, Why loose ye the colt? And they said, The Lord hath need of him. And they brought him to Jesus: and they cast their garments upon the colt, and they set Jesus thereon. And as he went, they spread their clothes in the way. And when he was come nigh, even now at the descent of the mount of Olives, the whole multitude of the disciples began to rejoice and praise God with a loud voice for all the mighty works that they had seen; Saying, Blessed be the King that cometh in the name of the Lord: peace in heaven, and glory in the highest. And some of the Pharisees from among the multitude said unto him, Master, rebuke thy disciples. And he answered and said unto them, I tell you that, if these should hold their peace, the stones would immediately cry out. And when he was come near, he beheld the city, and wept over it, Saying, If thou hadst known, even thou, at least in this thy day, the things which belong unto thy peace! but now they are hid from thine eyes. For the days shall come upon thee, that thine enemies shall cast a trench about thee, and compass thee round, and keep thee in on every side, And shall lay thee even with the ground, and thy children within thee; and they shall not leave in thee one stone upon another; because thou knewest not the time of thy visitation. (Luke 19:29–44 KJV)

All four gospel writers tell this story, the triumphant entry to Jerusalem on what we call Palm Sunday, to some degree. Of course, Luke tells us what the Pharisees were saying and what Jesus's response was—more of Paul's insight. And by the way, this portion is not recorded elsewhere.

Luke 19:45 through 21:36

Luke seems to follow the synoptic script through the Passion Week. Where is Saul? In his anger, I believe that he is working behind the scenes to secure the death of Jesus. If indeed he is the rich, young ruler, his hurt and disappointment with Jesus has come to a boil and he is seeking Jesus's life, not his teachings. Seeking his life was paramount—the culmination of the root of bitterness.

Then entered Satan into Judas surnamed Iscariot, being of the number of the twelve. And he went his way, and communed with the chief priests and captains, how he might betray him unto them. And they were glad, and covenanted to give him money. And he promised, and sought opportunity to betray him unto them in the absence of the multitude. (Luke 22:3–6 KJV)

Luke records an insight into what happened to Judas Iscariot that the others do not mention. Verse 3 says that Satan entered into Judas. This is an insight that may have been observed by Saul. In all the years of following the career of Jesus, Saul may have most closely identified with Judas. They both loved money! Matthew tells us that they gave Judas thirty pieces of silver and refers to Zechariah 11:12. Saul tells us about the fall of his friend, Judas.

Now before the feast of the passover, when Jesus knew that his hour was come that he should depart out of this world unto the Father, having loved his own which were in the world, he loved them unto the end. And supper being ended, the devil having now put into the heart of Judas Iscariot, Simon's son, to betray him; Jesus knowing that the Father had given all things into his hands, and that he was come from God, and went to God; He riseth from supper, and laid aside his garments; and took a towel, and girded himself. After that he poureth water into a bason, and began to wash the disciples' feet, and to wipe them with the towel wherewith he was girded. Then cometh he to Simon Peter: and Peter saith unto him, Lord, dost thou wash my feet? Jesus answered and said unto him, What I do thou knowest not now; but thou shalt know hereafter. Peter saith unto him, Thou shalt never wash my feet. Jesus answered him, If I wash thee not, thou hast no part with me. Simon Peter saith unto him, Lord, not my feet only, but also my hands and my head. Jesus saith to him, He that is washed needeth not save to wash his feet, but is clean every whit: and ye are clean, but not all. For he knew who should betray him; therefore said he, Ye are not all clean. So after he had washed their feet, and had taken his garments, and was set down again, he said unto them, Know ye what I have done to you? Ye call me Master and Lord: and ye say well; for so I am. If I then, your Lord and Master, have washed your feet; ye also ought to wash one another's feet. For I have given you an example, that ye should do as I have done to you. Verily, verily, I say unto you, The servant is not greater than his lord; neither he that is sent greater than he that sent him. If ye know these things, happy are ye if ye do them. I speak not of you all: I know whom I have chosen: but that the scripture may be fulfilled, He that eateth bread with me hath lifted up his heel against me. Now I tell you before it come, that, when it is come to pass, ye may believe that I am he. Verily, verily, I say unto you, He that receiveth whomsoever I send receiveth me; and he that receiveth me receiveth him that sent me. (John 13:1–20 KJV)

John tells us the intimate details of the paschal meal. Saul of Tarsus would not have been privy to this until many years later.

John Chapters 14–17

John fills in the details of the night of Passover. Saul is obviously not a party to any of this. Luke is silent.

And as soon as it was day, the elders of the people and the chief priests and the scribes came together, and led him into their council, saying, Art thou the Christ? tell us. And he said unto them, If I tell you, ye will not believe: And if I also ask you, ye will not answer me, nor let me go. Hereafter shall the Son of man sit on the right hand of the power of God. Then said they all, Art thou then the Son of God? And he said unto them, Ye say that I am. And they said, What need we any further witness? for we ourselves have heard of his own mouth. (Luke 22:66–71 KJV)

Luke tells us much more detail than Matthew or Mark. We have the inside report of the questions the priests, scribes, elders, and, most assuredly, the Pharisees asked of Jesus. Saul heard it all. Luke will also tell us what was done with the thirty pieces of silver in Acts 1:18–19.

And the whole multitude of them arose, and led him unto Pilate. And they began to accuse him, saying, We found this fellow perverting the nation, and forbidding to give tribute to Caesar, saying that he himself is Christ a King. And Pilate asked him, saying, Art thou the King of the Jews? And he answered him and said, Thou sayest it. Then said Pilate to the chief priests and to the people, I find no fault in this man. And they were the more fierce, saying, He stirreth up the people, teaching throughout all Jewry, beginning from Galilee to this place. (Luke 23:1–5 KJV)

Then led they Jesus from Caiaphas unto the hall of judgment: and it was early; and they themselves went not into the judgment hall, lest they should be defiled; but that they might eat the passover. Pilate then went out unto them, and said, What accusation bring ye against this man? They answered and said unto him, If he were not a malefactor, we would not have delivered him up unto thee. Then said Pilate unto them, Take ye him, and judge him according to your law. The Jews therefore said unto him, It is not lawful for us to put any man to death: That the saying of Jesus might be fulfilled, which he spake, signifying what death he should die. Then Pilate entered into the judgment hall again, and called Jesus, and said unto him, Art thou the King of the Jews? Jesus answered him, Sayest thou this thing of thyself, or did others tell it thee of me? Pilate answered, Am I a Jew? Thine own nation and the chief priests have delivered thee unto me: what hast thou done? Jesus answered, My kingdom is not of this world: if my kingdom were of this world, then would my servants fight, that I should not be delivered to the Jews: but now is my kingdom not from hence. Pilate therefore said unto him, Art thou a king then? Jesus answered, Thou sayest that I am a king. To this end was I born, and for this cause came I into the world, that I should bear witness unto the truth. Every one that is of the truth heareth my voice. Pilate saith unto him, What is truth? And when he had said this, he went out again unto the Jews, and saith unto them, I find in him no fault at all. (John 18:28–38 KJV)

These writers tell us that Pilate found "no fault in this man." John heard because he was following from afar. Saul had a front row seat. Luke then tells us in verse 5 that "he stirreth up the people." Saul knew the pandemonium. He may well have been leading the cheers, "Crucify him! Crucify him!" In Luke 23:6–12 is the insider knowledge of Jesus being sent by Pilate to Herod; it is not recorded elsewhere.

And, behold, two of them went that same day to a village called Emmaus, which was from Jerusalem about threescore furlongs. And they talked together of all these things which had happened. And it came to pass, that, while they communed together and reasoned, Jesus himself drew near, and went with them. But their eyes were holden that they should not know him. And he said unto them, What manner of communications are these that ye have one to another, as ye walk, and are sad? And the one of them, whose name was Cleopas, answering said unto him, Art thou only a stranger in

Jerusalem, and hast not known the things which are come to pass there in these days? And he said unto them, What things? And they said unto him, Concerning Jesus of Nazareth, which was a prophet mighty in deed and word before God and all the people: And how the chief priests and our rulers delivered him to be condemned to death, and have crucified him. But we trusted that it had been he which should have redeemed Israel: and beside all this, today is the third day since these things were done. Yea, and certain women also of our company made us astonished, which were early at the sepulchre; And when they found not his body, they came, saying, that they had also seen a vision of angels, which said that he was alive. And certain of them which were with us went to the sepulchre, and found it even so as the women had said: but him they saw not. Then he said unto them, O fools, and slow of heart to believe all that the prophets have spoken. (Luke 24:13–25 KJV)

Luke records the testimony of Pilate to the chief priests, rulers, and the people. These words still rang in Saul's ears.

Then the soldiers of the governor took Jesus into the common hall, and gathered unto him the whole band of soldiers. And they stripped him, and put on him a scarlet robe. And when they had platted a crown of thorns, they put it upon his head, and a reed in his right hand: and they bowed the knee before him, and mocked him, saying, Hail, King of the Jews! And they spit upon him, and took the reed, and smote him on the head. (Matthew 27:27–30 KJV)

And the soldiers led him away into the hall, called Praetorium; and they call together the whole band. And they clothed him with purple, and platted a crown of thorns, and put it about his head, And began to salute him, Hail, King of the Jews! And they smote him on the head with a reed, and did spit upon him, and bowing their knees worshipped him. (Mark 15:16–19 KJV)

Jesus is led away to be beaten and mocked, but Saul must still be inside the Praetorium. Luke says nothing.

And as they led him away, they laid hold upon one Simon, a Cyrenian, coming out of the country, and on him they laid the cross, that he might bear it after Jesus. And there followed him a great company of people, and of women, which also bewailed and lamented him. But Jesus turning unto them said, Daughters of Jerusalem, weep not for me, but weep for yourselves, and for your children. For, behold, the days are coming, in the which they shall say, Blessed are the barren, and the wombs that never bare, and the paps which never gave suck. Then shall they begin to say to the mountains, Fall on us; and to the hills, Cover us. For if they do these things in a green tree, what shall be done in the dry? And there were also two other, malefactors, led with him to be put to death. And when they were come to the place, which is called Calvary, there they crucified him, and the malefactors, one on the right hand, and the other on the left. (Luke 23:26–33 KJV)

Suddenly, as if Saul has caught up to the mob, we are told the things that Jesus says to the multitude. These statements are not found elsewhere.

³And when they were come to the place, which is called Calvary, there they crucified him, and the malefactors, one on the right hand, and the other on the left. Then said Jesus, Father, forgive them; for they know not what they do. And they parted his raiment, and cast lots. (Luke 23:33–34 KJV)

Luke, and Luke alone, records "Father, forgive them for they know not what they do." Saul was in the front row, able to hear. I can't help but believe that these words were particularly poignant to Saul. He would later say that His actions were in ignorance.

> And Jesus said unto him, Verily I say unto thee, Today shalt thou be with me in paradise. (Luke 23:43 KJV)

Only Luke records "Verily, I say unto thee, today shalt thou be with me in paradise."

> And when Jesus had cried with a loud voice, he said, Father, into thy hands I commend my spirit: and having said thus, he gave up the ghost. (Luke 23:46 KJV)

Mark and Matthew record that Jesus cried with a loud voice (Mark 15:37, Matthew 27:50). Only Luke records that Jesus said, "Father, into thy hands I commend my spirit"—the final words from the cross. John 19:30 records the sixth word, "It is finished," indicating that John was very close as well.

John does not record anything from the time that Jesus said, "Woman, behold, thy son! Then saith he to the disciples, Behold, thy mother! And from that hour the disciple took her unto his own home" (John 19:27). This indicates he left the scene and returned later after he had put Mary, the mother of Jesus, in his home. I think John gave Jesus the report, and He responded with, "It is finished" (John 19:30).

> (The same had not consented to the counsel and deed of them;) he was of Arimathaea, a city of the Jews: who also himself waited for the kingdom of God. (Luke 23:51 KJV)

Again, Luke records "inside" information that one would have had to be there to hear. "He had not consented to their counsel" refers to Joseph of Arimathaea. Saul was there when the decisions were made.

And, behold, two of them went that same day to a village called Emmaus, which was from Jerusalem about threescore furlongs. And they talked together of all these things which had happened. And it came to pass, that, while they communed together and reasoned, Jesus himself drew near, and went with them. But their eyes were holden that they should not know him. And he said unto them, What manner of communications are these that ye have one to another, as ye walk, and are sad? And the one of them, whose name was Cleopas, answering said unto him, Art thou only a stranger in Jerusalem, and hast not known the things which are come to pass there in these days? And he said unto them, What things? And they said unto him, Concerning Jesus of Nazareth, which was a prophet mighty in deed and word before God and all the people: And how the chief priests and our rulers delivered him to be condemned to death, and have crucified him. But we trusted that it had been he which should have redeemed Israel: and beside all this, today is the third day since these things were done. Yea, and certain women also of our company made us astonished, which were early at the sepulchre; And when they found not his body, they came, saying, that they had also seen a vision of angels, which said that he was alive. And certain of them which were with us went to the sepulchre, and found it even so as the women had said: but him they saw not. Then he said unto them, O fools, and slow of heart to believe all that the prophets have spoken: Ought not Christ to have suffered these things, and to enter into his glory? And beginning at Moses and all the prophets, he expounded unto them in all the scriptures the things concerning himself. And they drew nigh unto the village, whither they went: and he made as though he would have gone further. But they constrained him, saying, Abide with us: for it is toward evening, and the day is far spent. And he went in to tarry with them. And it came to pass, as he sat at meat with them, he took bread, and blessed it, and brake, and gave to them. And their eyes were opened, and they knew him; and he vanished out of their sight. And they said one to another, Did not our heart burn within us, while he talked with us by the way, and while he opened to us the scriptures? (Luke 24:13–32 KJV)

Luke records the story of two disciples on the road to Damascus, Cleopas and another.

There is very little information about this event. I surmise that this was one of those stories given to Luke from other sources. I also surmise that the story was in common circulation and Luke didn't have reason to question the authenticity of the narrative. For me, however, it paints the backdrop to the time that Jesus spent with the newly born-again Apostle Paul. Paul and Jesus may have had many of these walks and talks.

4

THE UNDOING OF THE MAN

Saul as a Tag-Along Pharisee

As I read the sections of Luke that are unique to Luke (that is, not found in the other gospels), I discovered what I consider a very important thing. I discovered that many of these passages dealt with the Pharisees from their point of view. It gives us a picture that is in harmony with the other gospels, but told from the point of view of an insider. Many of these additional stories or parts of stories may have been Paul's contributions because he was in the group. It seems to me that they begin fairly benign, then become increasingly more antagonistic. They move from curiosity to fear to anger to vitriolic cries for the death of Christ. That certainly seems to be true of the religious crowd in general and, more specifically as I see it, Saul of Tarsus. There seems to me to be one turning point where the view moves from curiosity and concern to malevolent determination to get rid of Jesus. To me, the turning point was twofold. First is when the rich, young ruler is embarrassed by Jesus and second is the resuscitation of Lazarus. One event was relatively private, the other was corporate and public. I believe that a "root of bitterness" sprung up within Saul of Tarsus, and he began to look for some way to avenge himself for what he considered public humiliation.

The biblical concept of the root of bitterness is first found in Deuteronomy 29.

> Lest there should be among you man, or woman, or family, or tribe, whose heart turneth away this day from the LORD our God, to go and serve the gods of these

nations; lest there should be among you a root that beareth gall and wormwood; And it come to pass, when he heareth the words of this curse, that he bless himself in his heart, saying, I shall have peace, though I walk in the imagination of mine heart, to add drunkenness to thirst: The Lord will not spare him, but then the anger of the Lord and his jealousy shall smoke against that man, and all the curses that are written in this book shall lie upon him, and the Lord shall blot out his name from under heaven. And the Lord shall separate him unto evil out of all the tribes of Israel, according to all the curses of the covenant that are written in this book of the law. (Deuteronomy 29:18–21 KJV)

We also find it in Hebrews.

Looking diligently lest any man fail of the grace of God; lest any root of bitterness springing up trouble you, and thereby many be defiled. (Hebrews 12:15 KJV)

The writer of Deuteronomy, Moses, warns against the man, woman, family, or tribe whose heart was turned away from the Lord God. He described the turning away as a turning to other gods which resulted in a root that bore gall and wormwood. The writer further indicates that such a person will heap unto himself or herself the curses of the covenant. Paul knew that he was guilty of such treachery. However, in 1 Timothy 1:13, he stated that he was given mercy because he did what he did in ignorance and unbelief. The root of bitterness can be anything that causes a person to become bitter, angry, or hurt enough to turn from the compassion of God and seek vengeance at any cost. In doing so, they turn their hearts away from God and focus upon the offense and the offender rather than upon the love of God. The writer of Hebrews, who I believe was Paul, picks up the narrative. He applies it to Christians who fail to utilize the grace of God and have the root of bitterness springing up within them, defiling them and the church.

Paul knew all too well that root of bitterness for it had consumed him and driven him to desire the death of this false messiah, Jesus.

Come with me as I describe for you that which I have seen as I studied this man, Saul. I saw him spying on Jesus. He listened but was unconvinced by the message of Jesus. The rising tide of resentment, fear, and hatred by his peers, the Pharisees, pulled at his heart. In the person of the rich, young ruler, it became personal. He, Saul, had sought to gain inside information by befriending one of Jesus's disciples, Judas Iscariot. He had heard Judas's frustration with Jesus's refusal to perform the expected role of a physical messiah who came to overthrow the Romans and finally rid the Jews of the intruders.

It is my opinion that what may have drawn Saul to Judas was their common weakness: the love of money. We know that Judas was the treasurer of the band of disciples and that he stole from the bag (John 12:6). The rich, young ruler had turned away from the Master's challenge to "sell all he had and come follow him." This common weakness planted the seed of a plot to gain vengeance upon Jesus. Saul encouraged Judas to seek out the chief priests and negotiate a price for betraying Jesus. In fulfillment of the Old Testament prophecy, they would offer Judas thirty pieces of silver, the price of a slave (Exodus 21:32).

Judas would not have known how to contact the chief priests, but Saul of Tarsus would. Saul was the insider who knew all the details of the deal. Saul of Tarsus was there when Judas brought the money back. Saul knew what was done with the blood money. Saul looks like a genius to the Pharisees and priests. He gets rid of the unwanted heretic, Jesus, and provides the money to buy a burial plot for those who were indigent. Saul comes out looking like a wonderful hero—a win-win situation. We are told by Paul in 2 Corinthians 11:14 that Satan masquerades as an angel of light. This is a good example. Saul's malignant intent seems to have no bounds.

Saul as the Rich, Young Ruler

In the blog *A Faith that Obeys*, Dana Haynes makes the argument that the Apostle Paul had met Jesus during the time that Jesus was conducting His earthly ministry. Haynes says that Paul may well have been the rich, young ruler.[9] I first heard this idea in seminary. I've spent a lifetime thinking about the idea. I think it is very possible that he was that young man. Looking at Mark 10:17–27, Matthew 19:16–22, and Luke 18:18–30 as my background, here are my reasons.

1.	He was young	Saul would have been young, less than thirty
2.	He was a ruler	Saul would have been considered a ruler because he was a member of the Sanhedrin
3.	He had kept the law from youth	Saul had kept the law from youth
4.	He had one sin that Jesus pointed out: his love of stuff	Paul said that the law slew him when it said thou shalt not covet; Paul loved stuff
5.	He went away sorrowing, most likely angry	Saul was angry, grief-stricken; after all, he had fulfilled the law, but it wasn't enough

This occurs in the latter Parean ministry of Jesus, not too long before the triumphal entry into Jerusalem.

Some may argue that there is not enough evidence in the New Testament to prove such a bold statement. I would argue that there is not enough evidence to disprove this assertion. Consider a psychological perspective that I have never seen discussed.

Why was Saul so angry? Why did he seek to destroy the infant church? What drove him to hold the coats of the men who stoned Stephen? I suggest that when Jesus confronted the rich, young ruler, He hit him with a gut punch that left him in complete shambles. Saul was a very proud, arrogant man whose entire stack pole of religion and self-worth revolved around the law. What he expected from Jesus was a commendation in front of a crowd. What Jesus did, what

---

9 Dana Haynes, "The Rich Young Ruler is Paul!," *A Faith That Obeys* (blog), July 10, 2020, https://www.afaiththatobeys.org/blog/the-rich-young-ruler-is-paul/.

Jesus always does, was speak truth into the rich, young ruler's world. It destroyed everything that Saul of Tarsus believed. In Saul's mind, what Jesus said just could not be true. Mark 10:22 says that he was sad and went away grieved. Part of the psychology of grieving is anger. When someone we love dies, our reaction is often anger. The other thing the passage says is that Jesus loved him (vs. 21). The hardest pills to swallow are hard things that are said by people who love us and know us.

Much of what we see in the book of Acts is Luke's explanation that Paul gave to him. I believe that the Apostle Paul had encountered Jesus of Nazareth, and it shook him to the core. There was no other way to deal with this angry young man. Not only were his eyes blinded that day but so was his view of theology and his understanding. Everything would have to heal. The healing, the discipleship, the formation of the greatest of the apostles began with utter blindness. Over a period of three years in the Arabian Desert, Paul would regain his physical sight and his spiritual perspective, a perspective that would change the world, and one that has changed so many of us.

John MacArthur tells how the book of Romans, written by the Apostle Paul, brought men like Augustine in AD 386 to Christ. In 1515, an Augustinian monk named Martin Luther came to Christ through Romans. On May 24, 1738, John Wesley was brought to Christ through reading the preface to the Epistle to the Romans by Martin Luther. William Tyndale was also brought to Christ through Romans.[10] God has used all of the Apostle Paul's writings to bring men and women to a saving knowledge of His Son, Jesus the Christ.

I wonder how many young men and women the Lord Jesus has stopped in their tracks. I've spent my life trying to be part of those events. If you've never been blinded by the light of truth, ask Jesus to come into your heart. He still saves! Oh, what a journey will begin in your life—a walk with the risen Lord!

---

[10] John MacArthur. "Romans: The Man and the Message", *Grace to You*. www.gty.org/library/sermons-library/45-01/romans-the-man-and-the-message, March 1, 1981

The Root of Bitterness

The "new" man in Christ, the Apostle Paul, was so 180 degrees from the "old" man, Saul of Tarsus. Saul of Tarsus was one angry dude. He was enraged by this messianic sect known as "The Way." After all, its leader and founder was the man who had shredded his theology in a public moment of embarrassment and humiliation. These "Christians," though I don't think they were called that just yet, were a continuing threat to the old-time religion of Saul's day. They were heretics. All his heroes agreed that they had to be eradicated. Saul saw men like Stephen as unpatriotic, anti-Israel, and as threats to the peace and comfort of the past most surely delivered to them by the prophets of old as recorded in sacred scripture. Somebody needed to do something. Why not him? Besides, it felt good to have the old ones applaud his zeal. "Go get them, Saul!" "Atta boy, Saul!" "You're the best, Saul!" "You're the man, Saul!" "Your folks must be so proud of you!" Youth and zeal plus anger and hurt form a powerful mixture that can drive a person to the verge of insanity. History is replete with so many examples: Hitler, Mussolini, Stalin, Mao, Hussein. Someone might ask, "Surely you aren't comparing the Apostle Paul to Hitler?" Yes, I am making that comparison, and I am suggesting that youth, zeal, anger, and hurt, if left unchecked, is a dangerous concoction that opens a person's life to limitless destructive potential. I don't know why God chose Saul of Tarsus and not Hitler or the like. All I do know is that the sovereign God of the universe does as He pleases. I thank God that He chose to change Saul into Paul. I thank God that he chose to call me as a ten-year boy in an R.A. camp in Big Spring, Texas. I do believe that Hitler and his ilk were given an opportunity by the living God to know His Son, but they rejected him. What a man, woman, boy, or girl does with God's invitation to accept His Son Jesus to be his or her Lord and Savior cannot be overstated as to their destinies, their eternal destinations.

I have tried to imagine what it must have been like for those relatively new believers in the infant churches in the first century. They were already enduring the persecution of their friends and family who remained unconverted Jews. Then, they heard that one Saul of Tarsus was coming to their town. He, Saul, had letters from the high priest in Jerusalem that they were to be captured and brought back to Jerusalem to stand trial. In some instances, they were to be killed on the spot because they dared to name the name of Jesus. F.F. Bruce, in his book, *Paul: Apostle of the Heart Set Free*, relates how the Sanhedrin still had power beyond Jerusalem and Judea. The Romans had granted Judea the status of sovereign state. A letter to Ptolemy VIII of Egypt in 142 BC concludes with the requirement, "If any pestilent men have fled to your country [Egypt] from their country [Judea], hand them over to Simon the high priest, that he may punish them according to their law" (1 Maccabees 15:21). Julius Caesar confirmed this power in 47 BC. It might be best described as a law of extradition. Saul bore such letters of extradition, and no one from "The Way" was safe from him. With great zeal, Saul persecuted the church (Philippians 3:6). Can you hear the shrieks of those being torn from their homes and families? Can you feel the terror the mere mention of the name Saul brought to every community? My mind sees the carnage left behind in the wake of this bloodthirsty, angry, bitter young man, Saul of Tarsus.

5

THE REBIRTH OF THE MAN

The conversion of Paul seems so simple at the outset. He was on his way to Damascus with letters of extradition. As he neared the city, he was engulfed in a light that was brighter than the sun at midday (Acts 22:6–13). Saul heard the voice of our Lord Jesus; his traveling companions did not, although they did see the light. Jesus spoke to Saul and said, "Saul, Saul, why persecutest thou me?" Saul wanted to make no mistake about what was happening, so he asked, "Who art thou, Lord?" I must say here that I think he recognized that voice. It was that same voice that he had heard so long ago, "Go sell all that you own and come follow me." For a split second, Saul must have thought, *Oh no, what is he going to do to me this time?* Instead, there is the question, "Why do you persecute me?" Jesus clearly identified himself as Jesus of Nazareth. There was no doubt in Saul's mind as to who had approached him. Saul had no confidence in the man from Nazareth. After all, "can anything good come out of Nazareth?" Now he was confronted by the risen, reigning Lord Jesus Christ. In that moment, Saul believed. The first time he addresses Jesus in Acts 22:8 as Lord, it is in polite speech. The second time he addresses Jesus, it is in the words of a servant: "What shall I do, Lord?" (Acts 22:10). The transition happened quickly. In that split second of faith, Saul became Paul. Saul was changed from the man breathing out murderous threats (Acts 9:1) to the humble, broken-hearted man who gave himself totally to Jesus.

Many years ago, on the streets of a town in Venezuela, I came to an open bar that was both part of a building and was also open to the sidewalk. I spoke to the bartender. I did what Dr. D. J. Kennedy has instructed in his book, *Evangelism Explosion*: I asked the man, "If you died tonight and stood before God, and He said to you, 'Why should I let you into my heaven?' what would you say?" He said, "I don't know." I asked him if he wanted to know what God said was the right answer. He said yes. I quoted from John's gospel, chapter 1, verse 12: "but as many as received Him, to them gave He the power to become the sons of God, even to them that believe on His name." The man replied, "I have always believed in Jesus." My response was that the devils in hell believe in Jesus, but an intellectual assent does not save them or anyone else. I told him that he must ask Jesus to come into his heart, give Jesus his life, and ask Him to save him and fit him for heaven. I asked him if he would like to pray a prayer and ask Christ into his heart. With my eyes looking directly into his, I led him in the sinner's prayer. The smile that came upon his face was more than I can describe. I like to think that on that Damascus road, the angry snarl of Saul of Tarsus was changed to the smiling face of the newly reborn Paul the Apostle. A sinner had come home, and by the grace of the Lord Jesus Christ, his sin was washed away, and a new life had begun. Oh, what a life it would be!

I am intrigued with those who ventured to help the man known as Saul of Tarsus, persecutor of "The Way." Ananias was the first to be called by God to this task. In a vision, Ananias was instructed to go to Judas's house on the street named Straight. I assume that Judas was one of Saul's contacts in Damascus, perhaps a fellow Pharisee. W.J. Brock wrote a beautiful essay/sermon on Ananias. He pictures a tugboat moving a massive ship out of port to open ocean. The tugboat, though vital, is slightly noticed compared to the grand ship. He compares Ananias to the tugboat. The Apostle Paul was the great ship.[11] On the day that God gave Ananias the vision to go to Judas's house, there was nothing grand or glorious about the Apostle Paul. He was just a blind man in need of healing, and Ananias was instructed to put his head in the lion's mouth, so to speak. Ananias was truly a reluctant tugboat. I cannot blame Ananias; I would have been, too.

God's words to Ananias were striking: "Go thy way…he, Paul, is a chosen vessel to me…to bear my name before the Gentiles, kings, and the children of Israel…for I will show him great things he must suffer for my name's sake" (Acts 9:15). I admire Ananias for his faithfulness.

---

[11]   W. Brock. "Ananias of Damascus." Biblehub. www.biblehub.com/sermons/auth/brock/ananias_of_damascus.htm., Accessed February 15, 2023.

I also find it intriguing that God chose to disclose to Ananias His plan for Paul. It is my experience that God seldom reveals to one His will for another.

Through Ananias's words, Paul received his direction. Through Ananias's hands, Paul received his sight, and the Holy Spirit filled Paul. Paul was immediately baptized. The Jews knew the baptism of proselytes, but Paul's baptism was a reversal of sorts. Paul moved from being the super Jew to the humble Christian. Can you imagine what Paul must have been thinking? If there ever was a conundrum, Paul was in the clutches of it. All his training, his life, his family, his hopes, his dreams—none of these things seemed to fit anymore. He had found Jesus; rather, Jesus had found him. He was being mentored by the Damascus church. He was preaching Christ as the Son of God. People were amazed.

Some say that Paul wasn't a great orator, but the presence of the Holy Spirit in him and on him, and a matchless testimony, was a powerful witness. They were amazed (Acts 9:15). However, Paul tells us that he needed and received more discipleship from the Lord Jesus Himself in the desert of Arabia (Galatians 1:12). The three years of discipleship reminds one of the three years that Jesus spent with His disciples. I think this reflects that Paul spent as much time with Jesus in his training, maybe more quality time, than Jesus did with the original apostles.

6

THE DISCIPLESHIP OF THE MAN

During Paul's sojourn in Arabia, what really happened? I believe the apostle had to reconcile his theological understanding with all that his new relationship with Jesus had brought to bear; from that comes the book of Romans. I believe that the apostle was preaching in the Arabian Desert, which is known as the Nabataean Kingdom. It was ruled by Aretas IV from 9 BC to AD 40. Aretas was probably the one who set a trap to catch the apostle on his last trip back to Damascus. He was rescued by some of the brothers in Damascus and let down over the wall in a basket. During that time, I believe that the book of Hebrews was developed, or at least the thought process that Jesus represented a superior priesthood and a superior covenant to that of the Old Testament. I will try to develop my thoughts on this idea later and propose the idea that at least Paul and Apollos, perhaps Dr. Luke, were all involved in the writing of the great apologetic book, Hebrews. I believe that Paul was required by God to surrender everything in his life that he held dear: his wife, his parents, his wealth, his station in the Jewish world, and even his health. Paul became a living sacrifice, perhaps as no other than his Lord and our Lord Jesus Christ. Romans 12:1–2 comes alive in this context. Ask Rick Warren. His book, *The Purpose Driven Life,* follows this thought as the singular premise for his book.

I find then, that Paul's discipleship during the three years in Arabia developed three distinct disciplines: his theological discipline, his preaching discipline, and his personal discipline. His subjection of his body with its will, emotions, passion, and weakness culminates in Romans, the seventh chapter, as his most difficult struggle. It is the thesis of this study that the struggles described in Romans 7 reach their climax in the verse that says, "Oh, wretched man that I am! who shall deliver me from the body of this death?" They move across the bridge of Romans 12:1–2, the bridge of the living sacrifice, that allows for the metamorphosis of the evil, ugly self into the spirit-filled beauty described in Romans 8, the spirit-filled world of no condemnation for those who walk not after the flesh but after the spirit. Paul ponders how one moves from the struggle of the flesh in Romans 7 to the victorious life in the spirit of Romans 8.

As Paul weaves together as close to a systemic theology as we have, I recall the story that Dr. Luke tells in his twenty-fourth chapter about the two men on the road to Emmaus. It records how the risen Jesus walked and talked with them, opened the Old Testament beginning with Moses, and showed them how the entire Old Testament applied to Himself. He set their hearts on fire with the clear understanding of what the truth of the Old Testament really was.

It was this same Jesus in the Arabian Desert who led Paul through the thoughts that we have in Romans. In one sense, Romans is not just a weaving together of Jewish and Christian thought. Paul ferrets out Jewish misunderstanding of Old Testament truths and introduces truth as presented by the author of the Old Testament and finisher of our faith, the Lord Jesus Himself. The human-made theology that had been developed by rabbis, scribes, Pharisees, and Sadducees, and the common theology of the Jewish people was set aside in the unveiling that is in Romans.

Old Testament truth stands clear in Romans; everything points to Jesus. I was taught in seminary that if we were to understand the Old Testament, we must read every passage and turn right to the cross, knowing that it all points to Jesus. Every time I have applied this teaching, my eyes have been opened to the blazing truths that are there. The Old Testament is not a dead, dull book. It is the living Word of the Father about His Son Jesus, the Christ. My pen has a hard time keeping up with my heart. I imagine that Paul must have felt something similar as the Holy Spirit moved him to recall and record the words of Jesus. I see them walking in the late evenings together, engaged in deep discussions. Again, I see them beside a crackling fire at night as every detail became clear. I hear the apostle asking questions, and the answers of Jesus striking like lightning bolts as "truth with no mixture of error" was conveyed to the great apostle. There is the rumble of thunder from Sinai as the Father encourages Paul by reminding him, "This is my beloved Son, hear him."

I believe the book of Romans is a brief summary statement of what the apostle heard from the Master. The revelatory truth of Romans is embedded in the revealed truth of the Old Testament. Some might remind me that it was the Holy Spirit that taught Paul. I would remind them that Paul talks about being caught up into the third heaven. I suggest the time of discipleship was very personal and very much a time of communing with the risen Lord. If, as I suspect, prayer brings us to the throne of God, and the Holy Spirit helps us pray, and our advocate, the great Savior of the sheep acts as the great high priest to bring those prayers to the Father, then the intensity of their time together was as close as anything in the three to three and a half years that Jesus spent with the original twelve. The richness of this time together is reflected in Paul's writing, his ministry, and his life.

Paul's struggles in the Arabian Desert were monumental. Discipleship begins with not so much an adding but rather a taking away—a "loosing." In the eleventh chapter of John is the beautiful story of the resuscitation of Lazarus. So many details in the story intrigue me, but one stands out to me in terms of discipleship. In that climactic moment when Jesus calls Lazarus from the tomb, the dead came forth, bound hand and foot with grave clothes. I've never been sure how Lazarus was able to walk or make his way to the door of that tomb. All I know is that he did. The next thing that Jesus says is my point here. Jesus says, "Loose him and let him go." I have come to believe over the years that the role of the church is the process of "loosing" the new Christian. Discipleship begins with taking away those things that will hinder one's growth as a Christian. The metamorphosis is to be aided by the church. This is what Paul received firsthand at the feet of the risen Lord.

Denny Burk, in an article entitled "Was the Apostle Paul Married?", argues that the word *unmarried* means those who have been married but now are unmarried for whatever reason: death, divorce, abandonment, whatever.[12] The logic is sound but doesn't go nearly far enough to hinge our case. Better scholarship includes arguments that suggest since Paul was most probably a member of the Sanhedrin, he was married because one of the requirements of being a member was to be married. Others, like F. F. Bruce, develop the view that Saul may have been married but that he gave it up because he "suffered the loss of all things" (Philippians 3:8). I believe Saul was indeed married, but when he became a Christian, his wife left him, deserted him. He would later argue that if the unbelieving mate cannot tolerate the believing mate due to his or her conversion experience, then the believer is allowed to "let them go" (1 Corinthians 7:15). This is a saying that comes from personal experience in my view. Were there children in his marriage? I think not. It would have made "letting them go" far more difficult.

The next struggle I think about was his relationship with his parents. Wayne Jackson, in an article in the *Christian Courier* entitled "Paul's Mother," says it is possible that, from the time of his Christian baptism, his Jewish family viewed him as a dead person, never to be mentioned in the domestic circle again. In effect, Paul was disowned by his father. This makes what Paul says in Romans 8:15 make sense: "For ye have not received the spirit of bondage again to fear; but ye have received the spirit of adoption, whereby we cry, Abba, Father."

At the time Paul wrote these words, and to some degree today, the law stipulated that a natural son may be disowned, but an adopted son may not be disowned. This was such a precious promise to Paul. Paul could cry "Abba, Father" without fear of being disowned. Paul gave up his earthly family for his spiritual family, his Heavenly Father.

In 1981, during the first Gulf War, it was my privilege to preach the Gospel in Nigeria. The whole nation of Nigeria went on alert as the tracers landed their green stripes upon Baghdad. I was in Kaduna (which means crocodile), the northern capital. We were on high alert because it was rumored that Saddam Hussein's wife was going to be sent to Kaduna. The last Sunday, I preached to one thousand people: "Ye must be born again." Five Muslim women walked the aisle to accept Christ as their Lord and Savior. Everyone in that congregation that

---

12   Wayne Jackson. "Paul's Mother", *Christian Courier*, www.christiancourier.com/articles/pauls-mother, Accessed February 2022

day was aware that they had just surrendered their whole lives. They had no family to return to—no husband, no children, no parents, no employment, nothing. Surely the great apostle would have understood their abandonment of everything for Jesus.

With the loss of his family also went the loss of his family fortune. This must have been particularly poignant to Paul. As with the rich young ruler, Paul probably had great wealth. Paul testifies in Romans 7:7, "What shall we say then? Is the law sin? God forbid. Nay, I had not known lust, except the law had said, 'Thou shalt not covet.'"

Paul had learned to live rich, and he soon learned to live poor (Philippians 4:12).

With his newfound salvation, Paul gave up his station in the Jewish nation as their rising superstar, their super Pharisee. He became an outcast to all those who had encouraged him in his search to destroy the Church of Jesus, The Way. As I watch politicians struggle today as they sell their souls for the sake of gaining political power, I realize that it was no small thing for Paul to surrender into Jesus's hand. All that had been was gone. Paul will tell us that he counted them as "dung" (Philippians 3:8).

Paul's total surrender to Jesus as Lord required him to enter a world of cruelty, harshness, spiritual warfare, and utter abject poverty at times. Does it not seem to you that the weakness of churches in general may well be due to the fact that we have not surrendered "everything" for Christ? Our "religion" is convenient, comfortable, and conjoined to the world in which we live. Listen to his testimony.

> Are they ministers of Christ? (I speak as a fool) I am more; in labours more abundant, in stripes above measure, in prisons more frequent, in deaths oft. Of the Jews five times received I forty stripes save one. Thrice was I beaten with rods, once was I stoned, thrice I suffered shipwreck, a night and a day have I been in the deep; In journeyings often, in perils of waters, in perils of robbers, in perils by mine own countrymen, in perils by the heathen, in perils in the city, in perils in the wilderness, in perils in the sea, in perils among false

brethren. ²⁷In weariness and painfulness, in watchings often, in hunger and thirst, in fastings often, in cold and nakedness. ²⁸Beside those things that are without, that which cometh upon me daily, the care of all the churches. (2 Corinthians 11:23–28)

Beyond all these things is the matter of Paul's "thorn in the flesh." At the outset of this discussion, I would like to say this to my Pentecostal friends. Your extreme mental gymnastics to avoid the obvious truth of this passage belies your inner conflict over your issues of God's sovereign right to rule His universe as He pleases. From the Pentecostal point of view, if a person asks God in faith to remove an illness, God is somehow obligated to do so. They will be quick to quote the verse found in James 5:15–17: "And the prayer of faith shall save the sick." Therefore, if one asks but does not receive healing, then it must be because he or she doesn't have enough faith. The dilemma is to say that the Apostle Paul lacked faith; surely that was not the case.

One plausible idea is that Paul must not be dealing with a physical illness; even though the passage says, "thorn in the flesh." Paul must have been using the phrase metaphorically. Perhaps Paul was talking about a Satanic spiritual foe because in 2 Corinthians 12:7–9, he refers to the "thorn" as a Satanic messenger, sent to keep him humble. In my judgment, there is no reason to go through such a mental test of agility to defend the false premise that "all sickness is from Satan."

I find that the sovereign God of the universe uses illnesses in four ways. Notice I didn't say *causes* illnesses.

1. God uses illness to bring punishment upon a person. The Old Testament is replete with numerous examples of such events. I would like to call your attention to Miriam, the sister of Moses, in Numbers 12. Miriam spoke ill of Moses in public because of his choice to marry an Ethiopian woman, a Cushite. In verse 10, we see that Miriam became leprous. She was put out of the camp (vs. 15). Moses interceded for her, and after seven days, she was healed and was admitted back into the camp.

Conclusion: God does use illness from time to time to bring His children back when they have sinned. In other words, God uses the illness that has come into this world to do a work in a person's heart for the purpose of redeeming that person. All things work together.

2. Is all sickness punishment for sin? No! In John's Gospel, chapter 9, there is the story of the man who was born blind. The disciples wanted to know why he was blind. After all, if all illness comes as punishment for sin, whose sin was it that caused his blindness, his parents or his own? Jesus's answer was startling then and is still startling to many today: "Neither this man nor his parents sinned, but this has happened so that the works of God would be displayed." Oh my. That means that the sovereign God of the Universe sometimes uses illness to demonstrate His power over all things. I have prayed for hundreds, if not thousands, of people and seen God do some pretty amazing things—but not always. God will not be bound by humans' misunderstanding of Scripture.

3. Thus far we have seen illness in two lives. God healed them both. With Miriam, it was after her repentance and Moses's intercession. With the man born blind, it was to draw attention to the power of God working in His Son, Jesus. Now we come to the third reason for illness: to maintain humility and usability in one of God's choicest servants, i.e., the Apostle Paul. The hands and faith of the apostle had brought healing to so many and even the raised the dead. Why would God not heal the great apostle? Many, many suggestions have been made as to what the *thorn* was. Maybe it was eye problems or epilepsy. It really doesn't matter. Like everything else, Paul had to lay it upon the altar and say to God the same thing our Lord said: "Nevertheless, not my will but thine be done."

4. The fourth reason for illness is that God uses it to take us home. Eternal death has been defeated by the resurrection of Jesus Christ. Physical death is as Forrest Gump's mother said: "just a part of life." Paul proclaims victory in 1 Corinthians 15:55–57.

O death, where is thy sting? O grave, where is thy victory? The sting of death is sin; and the strength of sin is the law. But thanks be to God, which giveth us the victory through our Lord Jesus Christ.

Many years ago in Santa Rosa, California, where I pastored, a wonderful lady named Willie Bollie lay in a coma in a local hospital. She had been diagnosed with kidney cancer, but for months she had hung on. I asked her husband, John, one Sunday morning how he was praying for her. He said, "I always pray for her healing." John was a small man but as tough as they came. He landed on every island in the Pacific as a marine in World War II. I asked him if he had ever prayed for God's will to be done for Willie. He admitted that he had not. That evening after church, we went to Willie's bedside in the small local hospital. As we laid hands on Willie and prayed, through tears that streamed down his face, John asked God to do that which was best for Willie. After we finished praying, John stayed in the room, but I headed down the long hallway and out the front door of the hospital. I was almost to my car when the nurse opened the door of the hospital and yelled to me, "She's gone." God had answered our prayers! As the Apostle Paul said in Philippians 1:21, "For me to live is Christ, and to die is gain." Willie received her healing and went to her reward in heaven. John found the peace of the Comforter in his heart that Willie was no longer suffering but safe in the arms of our Lord.

Some of Paul's greatest struggles were not of the physical sort; they were of the spiritual sort. The physical struggles were no doubt the arrows of Satan (2 Corinthians 12:7). However, Paul was learning in the desert that "we wrestle not with flesh and blood, but against principalities, against powers, against rulers of the darkness of this world, against spiritual wickedness in high places."

After much reading, I have come to the understanding that Jews in Paul's day did not believe too much in the evil one known as Satan. Much like people today, Satan was folklore. They claimed to be able to cast out evil spirits, but Jesus exposed them in Matthew 12:27 as frauds. Like much of the Christian world today, we wink at the idea of a devastating, demonic world. We toy with Halloween, tarot cards, horoscopes, and sordid stories like *The Exorcist*. After His baptism, the first place that Jesus went was into the wilderness to be tested/tempted by Satan. It is also fitting to understand that the apostle, as part of his discipleship, would come face to face with the spirit world and its ruler, Satan.

Some years ago, as I was ministering in Venezuela, I met a man named Gary Dawson. He told me a story about the conversion of a shaman of the Yanomami tribe known as Shoefoot because he was the first in his tribe to wear shoes. If you google Chief Shoefoot, you will find his story. Chief Shoefoot relates how he became a shaman and entered the spirit world. He drank the ground-up bones of his ancestors, took jungle types of drugs, and almost died. The purpose of the shaman supposedly was to protect the children of their village. In truth, they were responsible for the deaths of many, many children. He told about being in the spirit world and learning of God and Jesus. The demons told him how bad God was and that He had kicked them out of His heaven. When Dawson's parents first encountered Shoefoot, he spoke no English, and they did not speak Yanomami. They told him of Jesus in English; he heard in Yanomami. He was gloriously saved and rescued from the demonic.

Eventually he told Gary that in physical terms, Americans are giants (the Yanomami are short of stature), but in spiritual terms, Americans are dwarfs. That's how it must have been for the Apostle Paul. He became acquainted with the spirit world and grew to realize that the real warfare was not with "flesh and blood."

If one studies the psalms from the spirit world perspective, many of the psalms paint a picture of the demonic warfare that went on at the crucifixion of Jesus. Psalm 22 shows us the picture of Christ as He is on the cross, as He sees and feels it all. But many other psalms paint a picture of Satan's forces gathered on Golgotha. Bill Gaither pictures this in the song "It Is Finished."

> There's a line that's been drawn through the ages;
> On that line stands the old rugged cross.
> On that cross a battle is raging
> For the gain of man's soul or its loss.

On one side march the forces of evil,
All the demons and devils of hell;
On the other the angels of glory, and they meet on
Golgotha's hill.[13]

Satan certainly understood the psalms from the point of view that they referred to Jesus. Satan quotes Psalm 121:3 and Psalm 91:11–13, saying, "He will not allow thy foot to be dashed against a stone" (Luke 4:9–13). I am not defending Satan's exegetical prowess; I am simply stating that even the devil himself understood that all the Old Testament referred to Christ.

In the work that I have done in South America, especially Venezuela and Peru, I have come up against more overt forms of the demonic. In one crusade that we had in Puerta Ayacucho, Venezuela, we were made aware by local pastors of exorcisms that took place in the soccer stadium stands during the preaching of the Word and particularly during the invitation. My personal experience has been less overt and more of an awareness of great opposition to the work of the Holy Spirit.

On the first night of the crusade in Puerta Ayacucho, Venezuela, in the middle of their rainy season when they receive two hundred inches of rain on average for four months, the clouds rolled in, dark and ominous. The soccer field where we were meeting was beginning to be pelted by light rain. People in the stands were trying to seek shelter, but there was little to be had. I was sitting on a concrete barrier that protected the field from the running track that circled it. I put my head in my hands and began to pray, "Father, we came when You asked us to come; we have given our money, time, and energy to Your work. Nevertheless, this is not our crusade but Yours. If you choose to wash it out, so be it. Please do not let Satan get the glory!" When I opened my eyes, the clouds were parting. The rain went away like that each night of the crusade. I have pictures of the brilliant double rainbow that God gave us each night. We estimated that over 6,000 souls came to Christ. God got the glory—not me, not Satan. No one but God can part the clouds.

---

13   Gaither Vocal Band. "It Is Finished." *Reunited*. Spring House, 2009.

My friend Paul Lozuk was our point man in that crusade effort, and he faced the wiles of Satan far more than I. The week before the crusade began, a part went out on Paul's vehicle. An effort to find that part was made, but the part was not to be had in Venezuela at the time. Paul and I visited by phone about the problem. I was still in the U.S., and Paul was in Puerto Ayacucho. I searched using a computer and finally found the part in Chicago. I had it shipped to the place in Venezuela where Paul had his vehicle taken, about a day's journey from Puerto Ayacucho. Paul could not get there before our team was to arrive. It seemed that Satan had a won a tremendous battle.

Paul persevered through this unexpected hardship. However, God was at work. Satan would be defeated. The lady in charge of the soccer stadium was the sister of the wife of the governor of the area. She really was not terribly happy that we were using "her" soccer field. It had come down to us buying soccer shirts for all the kids who were learning to play soccer on that field. Several hundred shirts were donated, and we were able to use the field. The governor, his wife, and her sister were all devout Catholics. At the close of the crusade, the lady in charge of the soccer field came to Paul and me to tell us that her son was dying of cancer. She asked for prayers for him. He happened to live in the town where the part that Paul needed for his vehicle was.

The week after the crusade, Paul made the trek to the automobile place to pick up his car. While Paul was there, he went to see the young man who was dying with cancer. Paul led the young man to Christ. Hallelujah! The young man died a few short weeks later. Suddenly, we all understood that what Satan had meant for evil, God meant for good. The battle was won by the faithful partnership my friend Paul had with his God—our God. I believe that the Apostle Paul had many, many encounters with Satan of this magnitude and much greater. God was faithful. Satan was defeated. The Gospel spread like wildfire.

My point is this: the Apostle Paul went from being Satan's right-hand man to being perhaps one of his worst enemies. Paul's time in the Arabian Desert must have been a time of great testing, great spiritual warfare. I believe that Romans 7 is a picture of that warfare. The warfare was not only spiritual in nature, but also very, very personal, and very, very physical.

Let's look at Psalm 69. It is a psalm of David. It is autobiographical in nature and certainly describes how David must have felt at times. It also describes how Jesus must have felt on the cross. It is my belief that what happened to people of God in the Old Testament is condensed somehow into the suffering of Jesus on the cross of Calvary.

The psalm begins, "Save me, O God; for the waters are come in unto my soul" (vs. 1). Jesus is drowning in our sin, our judgment. His soul was overcome. He who knew no sin became sin for our sake. Verse 3 states, "I am weary of my crying; my throat is dried; mine eyes fail while I wait for my God." Part of crucifixion is the loss of bodily fluid. Jesus would cry out, "I thirst."

Verse 4 reads, "They that hate me without a cause are more than the hairs of mine head; they that would destroy me, being mine enemies wrongfully, are mighty." The combined forces of the Roman world and the Jewish world had come against Jesus, not to mention the devils of hell. Verse 6 states, "Let not them that wait on thee, O Lord God of hosts, be ashamed for my sake." Jesus is dying on an accursed tree. Paul will tell us about the fact that Jesus was a stumbling block, a cornerstone that the builders rejected. Verse 7 reads, "Because for thy sake I have borne reproach; shame hath covered my face." Jesus hung naked before the world.

Verse 8 reads, "I am become a stranger unto my brethren, and an alien unto my mother's children." In Mark 3:21, Jesus's mother and brethren thought He was insane and sought to take Him home. When He knew that they were seeking him, He asked, "Who is my mother… who are my brethren?" Surely, for a while Jesus was a stranger to His family. He was certainly a stranger to the commonwealth of Israel. He came unto His own, and His own knew Him not (John 1:11).

"For the zeal of thine house hath eaten me up; and the reproaches of them that reproached thee are fallen upon me" (Psalm 69:9).

"And God laid upon Him the iniquity of us all" (Isaiah 53:6).

"And hide not thy face from thy servant; for I am in trouble: hear me speedily" (Psalm 69:17).

"My God, my God, why hast thou forsaken me?" (Psalm 22:1).

Verse 20 of Psalm 69 reads, "Reproach hath broken my heart; and I am full of heaviness: and I looked for some to take pity, but there was none; and for comforters, but I found none." Jesus died of a broken heart, literally and figuratively. Verse 21 reads, "They gave me also gall for my meat; and in my thirst they gave me vinegar to drink." They gave Him vinegar to drink mixed with gall (Matthew 27:34).

From the psalmist's writings, we see the crucifixion from the cross, from Jesus's perspective. My opinion is that we get to experience the agony of the cross through what the psalmist (i.e., the Holy Spirit) records.

In the gospels, we see the crucifixion from the point of view of the apostles who watched Him die. From the psalms, we see His death from His eyes. We see Satan and his legions tormenting our Lord. The Apostle Paul in the Arabian Desert would experience some of that torture and torment, but he would also have the Holy Spirt to comfort him and teach him. I believe that Jesus Himself told Paul what He had felt, what the warfare was like. Is it any wonder that Paul fell more and more in love with Jesus every day and was willing to suffer for Jesus's sake because Jesus had suffered for him, for us?

Let's look at Paul's great struggle in Romans 7:7–25.

Verse 7 states, "What shall we say then? Is the law sin?" I can still hear my Greek professor, Dr. Ray Ellis, almost screaming Paul's answer, "God forbid!" In Greek, that is "not never at no time." Bad English, but good Greek. The law served the purpose of shining the spotlight on sin, pointing it out, identifying it. To that end, the law is good.

Verse 8 states, "But sin, taking occasion by the commandment, wrought in me all manner of concupiscence." The law made Paul aware of just how sinful he was. He would not have known otherwise.

Verse 9 states, "For I was alive without the law once: but when the commandment came, sin revived, and I died." Paul was innocent before he knew the law, but when he understood the law, he died. He sinned; he broke the law. The wages of sin is death (Romans 6:23).

Verse 10 states, "And the commandment, which was ordained to life, I found to be unto death." The commandment, the law, designed to protect humans from sin, became that which condemned him.

Verse 11 states, "For sin, taking occasion by the commandment, deceived me, and by it slew me." "Thou shalt not" killed our grandparents in the garden. Its provocative nature laid a trap for Paul and killed him, too.

Verse 12 reads, "Wherefore the law is holy, and the commandment holy, and just, and good." Paul acknowledges that the fault is not the law's for it is holy and good.

Verse 13 reads, "Was then that which is good made death unto me? God forbid." Was it the law's fault that Paul was a sinner? Here's that double negative in Greek again translated as "God forbid."

Verse 14 reads, "For we know that the law is spiritual: but I am carnal, sold under sin." The law is a spiritual tool of God for our good. The problem is humanity. Human beings are sinners, inheriting the weakness to sin. Paul identifies the weakness as carnal, fleshly.

Verse 15 reads, "For that which I do allow not: for what I would, that do I not; but what I hate, that do I." My carnal nature is such that I know better than to do things, but I do them anyway. It makes me hate myself.

Verse 16 reads, "If then I do that which I would not, I consent unto the law that it is good." I must admit that everything the law says is good; therefore, the law is good.

Verse 17 reads, "Now then it is no more I that do it, but sin that dwelleth in me." It seems that my carnal nature takes over my weakness, and I can't stop myself from sinning. Sin indwells our very being.

Verse 18 states, "For I know that in me (that is, in my flesh,) dwelleth no good thing; for to will is present with me; but how to perform that which is good I find not." Paul was convinced that the weakness of flesh was the evil from within that had corrupted everything including his very will. In his flesh, even his best efforts to do good were failures.

In verse 19, we read, "For the good that I would I do not: but the evil which I would not, that I do." When I know the good, I do the evil.

Verse 20 states, "Now if I do that I would not, it is no more I that do it, but sin that dwelleth in me." This awful weakness, this sinfulness, dwells in me.

Verse 21 reads, "I find then a law, that, when I would do good, evil is present with me." The law of my flesh is this: I try to do good, but my weak sinful nature is always there to keep me from it.

In verse 22, we read, "For I delight in the law of God after the inward man." My inward nature, my spiritual nature, really wants to do good; I really want to.

Verse 23 reads, "But I see another law in my members, warring against the law of my mind, and bringing me into captivity to the law of sin which is in my members." I now understand that I am a captive to sin. I am held by chains of my own flesh.

Verse 24 states, "O wretched man that I am! who shall deliver me from the body of this death?" We must camp out on this verse for a moment. From many years ago comes a haunting picture of what Paul is saying. It seems that it was a common practice in Paul's day to punish a political prisoner by taking a dead body from the arena and strapping or chaining that rotting, stinking corpse to the prisoner face to face. The corruption of the decaying flesh would soon penetrate the healthy flesh of the prisoner. Death of the most horrible nature would soon occur. This is an unthinkable picture, but its power to let us hear the heart of Paul, and most surely the heart of God, is undeniable.

I, myself, have known Paul's struggles. I believe that every truthful Christian will attest that he or she has not been able to live the Christian life in his or her flesh. Every morning, the old man, my flesh, rises with me. Every day there is the struggle. I think that the Great Apostle had been comfortable in his ignorance concerning the true nature of sin. He had been a proud Pharisee. He had been confident of his position in God as a true Hebrew, chosen of God, special, elite. As the rich, young ruler, as the fire-breathing Saul, he was comfortable. But when he met Jesus, He came face to face with the reality of his own sinfulness. The old proverb (23:7) echoed through his mind: "As a man thinketh in his heart, so is he." Was there any hope?

In verse 25 of chapter 7, the lightning flashes: "I thank God through Jesus Christ our Lord. So then with the mind I myself serve the law of God; but with the flesh the law of sin." Through the death, burial, and resurrection, he could be saved. By the power of Christ, he could find victory over his weaknesses. While he still sinned, in him dwelt the eternal God who was forgiving him, transforming him, making him a new man, a spiritual man, daily. We read in Romans 8:1, "There is therefore now no condemnation to them which are in Christ Jesus, who walk not after the flesh, but after the Spirit." I love the version of the song "Amazing Grace (My Chains Are Gone)" by Chris Tomlin. Tomlin sings, "My chains are gone, I've been set free, / My God, my Savior has rescued me. / And like a flood His mercy reigns, / unending love, / amazing grace."[14] The great apostle has found the cure for his sin—God's amazing grace—in the shed blood of Jesus.

I think in the sands of the Arabian Desert, Paul came to grips with the awfulness of sin and the awesomeness of God's grace. I can feel his love for Jesus growing with every breath he breathed. I can also feel the continuing struggle with his flesh.

The eighth chapter of Romans is arguably the high-water mark of everything the apostle wrote. In it he pictures the spirit-filled life, the victorious life. Look at verse 10, which reads, "And if Christ be in you, the body is dead because of sin; but the Spirit is life because of righteousness." Keep reading on to verse 15, which states, "For ye have not received the spirit of bondage again to fear; but ye have received the Spirit of adoption, whereby we cry, Abba, Father." All of Paul's pain regarding his earthly family and being disowned by his earthly father have simply dissolved into the truth that his Heavenly Father had chosen and adopted him. He could never be disowned again. He, and we, are now joint heirs with Christ (vs. 17). The treasure house of Heaven has been opened to Paul and all those who have been born again.

In verse 18, Paul shares how he viewed the sufferings of Sinai. They were not worthy to be compared with the glory which shall be revealed in us. Verse 22 says the whole universe is in eager anticipation of the coming end of the age.

In verse 28 (many people's favorite verse), Paul tells us of his conviction that every struggle, every surrender, every inner pain, every dashed dream was being woven into the tapestry of life for the good of the child of God. Everything is proceeding from the plan of God—His foreknowledge of all things, His agreement to give humans free will, His foreknowledge to save all who receive the Lord Jesus.

---

14 Tomlin, Chris. "Amazing Grace (My Chains Are Gone)", *See the Morning*, Ed Cash, 2006

In verse 33, Paul answers the charges of Satan, our adversary, our accuser, saying, "Who shall lay anything to the charge of God's elect? It is God that justifieth." Paul's guilt was lifted; the victory over Satan was complete. Paul understood what the forgiveness of sin really meant: a cleansed conscience before God. Nothing could or can change that. Nothing, I tell you, nothing, as verses 35 through 38 indicate. Satan tried to destroy Paul in the desert, but through the power of the Holy Spirit and the personal walk with Jesus, Paul found what I call a bridge from the fleshly life to the spirit-filled life.

The bridge is most clearly explained in Romans 12:1–2. These verses are Paul's definition of worship. I am convinced that what we have labeled as worship is not, at least by Paul's standards. We often think of music as worship, or the preaching as worship. Some think of a sunrise as worship or some glory in nature. By Paul's definition, true spiritual worship is completely different.

> I beseech you therefore, brethren, by the mercies of God, that ye present your bodies a living sacrifice, holy, acceptable unto God, which is your reasonable service. And be not conformed to this world: but be ye transformed by the renewing of your mind, that ye may prove what is that good, and acceptable, and perfect, will of God. (Romans 12:1–2 KJV)

The secret to the spirit-filled life is worship, total complete surrender upon the altar of our hearts, for our bodies are the temples of the indwelling God. As living sacrifices, we surrender *all* our rights. That is exactly what empowered the great apostle. He gave God everything and lived his life in that state of surrender.

The importance of this principle cannot be overstated. As a pastor, I struggled with trying to live the victorious life. My congregation struggled with the daily reality of trying to overcome the flesh. I loved the title of Erma Bombeck's book *If Life Is a Bowl of Cherries, What Am I Doing in the Pits?* I have heard preachers say that "we can't live the Christian life; only Christ can." I agree with that, but how can we let

Him live His life in us? From the depths of Paul's struggles comes a simple formula.

In an attempt to make the principle of a living sacrifice abundantly clear, I have outlined Romans 12:1–2. Please consider the following outline. I believe it will revolutionize your walk with the Lord. I have also mentioned the great baptismal hymn that Paul included in Philippians 2:5–11. Paul and Silas sang that song, perhaps, at midnight in the Philippian jail. It was truly a moment of worship—so much so that God rocked the prison and set them free. True spiritual worship always sets us free.

1. Present your body (flesh) to God as a living sacrifice.

2. Dare to let Him (God) take out anything that doesn't fit, including,

   a. Your job;
   b. Your hopes; and
   c. Your dreams.

   Nothing is off limits

3. Surrender all your rights:

   a. The right to be comfortable;
   b. The right to be appreciated;
   c. The right to be moved to another place; and
   d. Anything that is a right.

   A sacrifice has no rights

4. Be willing to be different and set apart for God.

5. In the process of surrendering your life, you become acceptable to God.

6. This is spiritual worship.

7. The results of total surrender are the following.

   a. You will not be like the world around you.
   b. You will be transformed, experience metamorphosis like the caterpillar changes to a butterfly.
   c. Your mind will be renewed, as stated in Philippians: "Let this mind be in you, which was also in Christ Jesus: who made himself of no reputation, and took upon him the form of a servant" (Philippians 2:5–11 KJV).
   d. Christ became obedient to God so much that He obeyed His Father's will to die upon the cross, wherefore, God hath highly exalted Him.
   e. If you surrender all to God, God will give you a name: faithful.
   f. God receives great glory when we follow Paul's formula.

A word of warning needs to be stated here. Satan wants anything and everything but this type of surrender for your life. The warfare—spiritual warfare—will be more than you can handle on your own. You will need to put on the full armor of God (Ephesians 6:11–18).

Imagine with me the discussion by the evening fire between Jesus and Paul. Paul says, "Lord, when I crawl on the altar to become the living sacrifice, I feel that I am the most vulnerable. Satan comes at me with everything he has." Our Lord shows Paul the vision of the Roman soldier prepared for battle, a figure that would have been very familiar to the Great Apostle and all the rest of the world in that day. The analogy will find its way into the letter to the Ephesians, chapter 6, verses 10 through 19. Except for the moment in the Arabian Desert, it is our Lord's preparation of the apostle to be the greatest spiritual general of the human condition.

"Paul," Jesus said, "the first place Satan will always try to attack you is your heart." The ancient words of Solomon may have flooded into Paul's mind: "For as a man thinketh in his heart, so is he" (Proverbs 23:7). Paul would have understood that his heart was the center of his spiritual universe. As David had cried out in Psalm 51:10, "Create in me a clean heart, O God; and renew a right spirit within me." The living sacrifice was the process of the creation of the clean heart. To protect that process from the assault of Satan, Paul would need the equivalent of a breast plate, a spiritual breast plate of imputed righteousness. Again, King David speaks from his own surrender to God in Psalm 32:2: "Blessed is the man unto whom the Lord imputeth not iniquity, and in whose spirit there is no guile." Satan's attack on the surrendered heart is to accuse the living sacrifice of his or her forgiven sin. Satan's name means *accuser*. Paul realizes this truth, states it in Romans 8:1–17: "There is therefore now no condemnation to them which are in Christ Jesus." The righteousness of Christ protects a Christian heart, because "Who shall lay anything to the charge of God's elect? It is Christ that died, yea rather, that is risen again, who is even at the right hand of God, who also maketh intercession for us" (Romans 8:33–34). Paul assures us that *nothing* can separate us from our heart relationship with God (Romans 8:38-39). "If you are in Christ, Paul, your heart is mine, forever shielded by the righteousness of Jesus Christ." Can you hear the apostle shouting for joy?

However, in the midst of his euphoria, the apostle is reminded that the living sacrifice must be tried in the dusty streets of human existence. The small villages of the Arabian Desert were filled with all manner of desperately defiled human refuse who would seek to douse the fires of the altar on which Paul had laid his life. Paul asks, "How, Lord, can I go into such sewers of humanity and keep my soul surrendered before You?" Jesus turns the apostle's attention to the boots (*caligae*) that the Roman soldiers of his day wore. John MacArthur makes a profound point in a sermon he preached on this subject. Ephesians 6:15 primarily addresses the Christian's fight with Satan. The Roman boot was designed to assure one's ability in his or her fight with the enemy. The boots were hobnailed, according to Wikipedia, much like the cleats on athletic shoes.[15] MacArthur's point is that the shoes did not represent the spread of the Gospel through evangelism. Rather, they represent the ability to resist Satan, to stand in the face of the adversary, to hold

---

[15] John MacArthur. "The Armor of God: The Shoes of the Gospel of Peace and the Shield of Faith", Grace to You, www.gty.org/library/sermons-library/90-366/the-armor-of-god-the-shoes-of-the-gospel-of-peace-and-the-shield-of-faith, November 16, 2008

one's ground, to not give in or give up.[16] As Paul writes, "That ye may be able to withstand in the evil day, and having done all, to stand" (Ephesians 6:13).

"Paul," Jesus said, "You are no longer an enemy of God the Father; we are on your side." Remember Romans 5:10, which reads, "For if, when we were enemies, we were reconciled to God by the death of his Son, much more, being reconciled, we shall be saved by his life." The exclamation point of this thought is expressed in Romans 8:31: "What shall we then say to these things? If God be for us, who can be against us?" The Holy Spirit encouraged Paul, "In all these things we are more than conquerors through him that loved us" (Romans 8:37).

So much of what we see in the victory chapter of Romans 8 relates directly to the armor prescribed in Ephesians 6. We can only win the victory when we have worshiped in spirit and truth and put on the whole armor of God. After the many years I have pastored, I am convinced that I often sent my congregation back into the world to face the fiends of Satan unprepared. Either I did not help them worship as living sacrifices or I had not understood that our purpose as pastors is to help our congregants put on the spiritual armor for the battle. Forgive me, Lord!

I believe that Jesus encouraged Paul to take up his shield of faith. The Roman shield was different from most shields. In the movie *Gladiator*, the shields that the gladiators used were those that the Roman legions used. They were about three and a half feet tall and about three feet across. The vertical edges curved so that they didn't stop the arrows of the enemy, but rather they deflected them. The shield is the first line of defense; it was used from the very inception of the battle to ward off all the fiery darts and poison arrows of the enemy. Paul would have understood that the faith in his heart was his first opportunity to deflect the temptations of Satan. Satan comes from all directions to try to injure the Christian's heart and soul. Inside the shield is a knob that was simply called the "boss." The "boss" allowed the soldier to move the shield to the place of attack. I believe that prayer is the "boss" that implements the power of the Holy Spirit to move the shield to the point

---

16

of the enemy's attack. In Romans 8:24–27, Paul reiterates what our Lord explained to him.

> For we are saved by hope: but hope that is seen is not hope: for what a man seeth, why doth he yet hope for? But if we hope for what we see not, then do we with patience wait for it. Likewise the Spirit also helpeth our infirmities: for we know not what we should pray for as we ought: but the Spirit itself maketh intercession for us with groanings which cannot be uttered. And he that searcheth the hearts knoweth what is the mind of the Spirit, because he maketh intercession for the saints according to the will of God.

In *Star Wars*, there is an interesting scene as the young Luke Skywalker seeks to become a Jedi knight. Obi Wan instructs him with a device that can hurl an electronic impulse from any direction. The Jedi is supposed to use the "force" to know and anticipate where the attack will be coming from and adroitly move his light saber into place to deflect the charge. So sure is Obi Wan of the force's ability to protect the Jedi that he puts a helmet on Luke that prevents him from using his eyes. This makes Luke have to "use the force."

The story, though fiction, illustrates the point here. We do not believe in some animistic force that exudes from all living things. We do believe in the Holy Spirit who fills all believers. As the believer prays, he or she unleashes the Holy Spirit, who in turn aids the believer to position his or her shield of faith to deflect the darts of Satan. When we try to face Satan with our fleshly eyes, we find ourselves victims, but the Spirit gives us victory. Paul was learning. He was learning to rely on the Spirit. Paul's faith allowed him to stand in a world of constant battle against our arch enemy and all his minions.

"But Lord Jesus," Paul might have asked, "it's my mind that is so easily attacked by Satan." I hear the Master remind Paul that as the living sacrifice yields himself or herself before the Father, he or she is transformed and his or her mind is renewed (Romans 12:2). Paul might also have asked, "But Lord, what does it mean to have a 'renewed' mind?" Can you see a smile cross the Master's face?

"Well, brother Paul, you must have my mind."

As I have said, Paul will later write in Philippians 2:5, "Let this mind be in you, which was also in Christ Jesus."

"Wow, Lord! Is it possible to think like You think?"

"Yes! Paul, the Spirit will lead you into all truth. My mind is truth and love. Your living sacrifice will be like my sacrifice when I thought it not robbery to be equal with the Father. I made myself of no reputation, and took upon myself the form of a servant and was made in the likeness of humans. And being found in fashion as a man, I humbled myself and became obedient unto death, even death of the cross. My Father has exalted me and given me a name which is above every name. The day is coming, Paul, when every knee shall bow, in Heaven and in earth and under the earth, the day will come when every tongue will confess that I am the Lord. And everything I do is to the glory of God the Father" (Philippians 2:6–11).

"Oh Jesus, I want your mind. I want to think like you think."

Jesus replies that the living sacrifice is the beginning place for the victorious Christian life that we live by the power of the Holy Spirit.

The helmet of salvation protects our minds and helps us deal with Satan's accusations of past failures and haunting fears that he uses to incapacitate us. Paul reminds Timothy in 2 Timothy 1:7, "For God has not given us the spirit of fear; but of power, and of love, and of a sound mind." The helmet of salvation is the ever-present Holy Spirit of God allowing us to be sane in an insane world. Salvation is God's power in us to overcome Satan with truth and overcome the world with God's love. The helmet of salvation protects us from Satan's sword, a sword that attacks us with discouragement and doubt. Our salvation has brought us into the confident hope that God is able to do all that He has promised. When Satan hits us with doubt, the helmet deflects his blow with hope. In the first letter to the Thessalonians, chapter 5, Paul called the helmet "the helmet of the hope of salvation."

Do you think that the Apostle Paul ever became discouraged or had doubts? I do. I believe that Satan attacked him with all the fury of hell. Paul faced every kind of thing that would cause discouragement. He was beaten. He was imprisoned. He was shipwrecked. He was bitten by a snake. He was laughed at. He was rejected in every way, but the helmet of salvation kept his mind stayed on the Lord.

Do you think that the Apostle Paul ever had any doubts? This is one of Satan's favorite tactics. Paul could have doubted the promises of God in that Philippian jail at midnight, his hands and feet in chains, his back striped from the lashes of the whip (Acts 16:33). It's dark, it's really dark. Can you hear Satan whisper in his ear, "Where is your God now, Paul? You've bought into a hoax." As I continue to say, the Holy Spirit reminded him of God's faithfulness in the past and His promise for the future. Instead of losing hope, he began to sing the baptismal hymn found in Philippians 2:5–11. It is no wonder that God answered with an earthquake, set his adopted son free, and gave him souls (the jailor and his whole family) for his hire. Thank God for the helmet of salvation that protects our renewed minds.

"But Lord," Paul may have said, "I don't want to simply stand there. I want to attack Satan. How is that possible? He's not flesh and blood. He is a spirit."

Jesus's answer would have been clear. "When I was tested by Satan in the wilderness, he came at me with twisted scripture. I answered him with truth that was rightly divided, not twisted, scripture. He left me. Your sword, Paul, is scripture, rightly divided and properly interpreted by the Holy Spirit. In truth, it will be the Spirit that does battle with Satan in your body." Truly, the scripture is the sword of the Lord. Our success will depend upon our spiritual preparation which comes through prayer, watching for Satan's attacks, and persevering as we link our arms with other saints in the same battle. It is not just us that Satan is after. He seeks to devour everyone in his path like a roaring lion.

Let us see a composite of the great apostle. He began life like his namesake, Saul, the first king of Israel. Saul of Tarsus had some of the same character flaws as King Saul had; both needed the approval of others. In that regard, they were "little" men, though King Saul was "head and shoulders taller than any other man in Israel." King Saul was so jealous of the shepherd boy named David that he sought to kill him on numerous occasions. The women of Israel had a song that said, "Saul has killed his thousands, but David has killed his ten thousands." Saul's relationship with Samuel demonstrates that Saul needed the word of Samuel to keep him on top of things. Both King Saul and Saul of Tarsus seemed to have a problem of self-perception. If, as I have surmised, Saul of Tarsus is the "rich, young ruler," the need for Jesus's approval stands clear. The words of Jesus, not unlike the words of Samuel, did not provide the necessary "ego boost." My vision of King Saul is that he was a large man physically, but a small man psychologically and spiritually. My vision of Saul of Tarsus is similar, though we get no indication the Saul of Tarsus was large in stature. As a matter of conjecture, I think Saul of Tarsus may have been small in stature. He seems to have had the "little man" syndrome. Nevertheless, both King Saul and Saul of Tarsus were little men in terms of their psychological makeup. When Jesus confronted the rich, young ruler, suggested he sell all his possessions, give the proceeds to the poor, and follow Him, the rich, young ruler went away sorrowing, for he loved the things of this world more than he loved God. A similar story is Samuel's instructions to King Saul about the total Jehad fleet that was to be delivered against the Kenites. Saul kills everyone but their king and their livestock. Saul loved the things more than he loved God.

While Saul of Tarsus would have been dwarfed by King Saul's armor as David was, Paul the apostle of the Lord Jesus Christ, stood taller than the giant Goliath when he put on the whole armor of God. I submit to you that Paul the apostle stood head and shoulders above all others as the spiritual warrior of the living God. Paul's sojourn in the desert of Arabia had given him the opportunity to grow into the armor of God.

"Lord, it is so difficult to know heresy from what is good and right. Satan packages his lies in near truths."

"Yes, Paul, the beginning of defeating Satan is like the great belt that a Roman soldier wears (Ephesians 6:10–20). The belt represents truth—the immutable, unchangeable truth."

"Lord," Paul says, "I spent my life thinking that I knew the truth, but alas, I only knew small pieces of truth that were often muddled by the Pharisees and Sadducees."

I hear the voice of our Lord softly say to Paul, "You know, Pilate asked me a question when I stood before him. He asked, 'What is truth?'

Paul, I am the way, the truth, and the life. The more you know me, the more you will know the truth. You will know the truth, and the truth will set you free, even when Satan is doing everything he can to bind you. Truth is central in everything you do or think in the days ahead." Jesus added, "Everyone who is of the truth hears my voice. The Holy Spirit will guide you into all truth (John 16:13). My prayer for you, Paul, is that you will be sanctified by truth, for the Word of God is truth" (John 17:17).

I remember words from Herschel Hobbs, heard so long ago in a seminary class at Golden Gate Seminary. He said, "The Bible is God's Word with no mixture of error." He was quoting from the Baptist Faith and Message, 1963 confession, a piece that was long used by Baptists as an expression of those things most surely believed by Baptists. Dr. Hobbs chaired the committee that put the Statement of Faith together.

7

THE GREAT APOSTLE PAUL

Out of the Arabian Desert, after three years of discipleship, emerged the greatest missionary of all time. He was battle-hardened from the warfare against Satan. I believe that no one else ever battled Satan as much as the Apostle Paul except for our Lord Jesus Christ. For the next decade, Paul sought out those who had not heard the Gospel from Jerusalem to Illyricum (Romans 15:17–21). He was intentionally going to those who had not heard for he did not want to build upon another man's foundation. In fact, as many scholars agree, his preaching was so effective in the regions that the Nabataean Arab ruler, Aretas, was trying to capture him as he was visiting Damascus. The plot was uncovered by several of Paul's brethren; they let him down over the wall of Damascus in a basket, and he escaped capture. Josephus records a war between King Aretas and his former son-in-law, Herod Antipas. Aretas saw Paul perhaps as a trouble-making ally of Herod Antipas. [17] Political and religious unrest would have been met with serious consequences. Paul was never quiet; he was ever preaching Jesus. He could seldom stay in the same place long. Can you see this vibrant preacher, itinerant no doubt, entering the little villages from Jerusalem to the west side of Greece and Illyricum? Thousands, if not hundreds of thousands, of people heard the Gospel from the lips of Paul. These thirteen or so years were spent telling the story, all before we knew him as the great missionary and years before his stay in Antioch.

---

[17] F.F. Bruce. *Paul: Apostle of the Heart Set Free*. Grand Rapids, MI: Wm. B. Eerdmans Publishing Co., 1977, 72

Emil Brunner once said, "A church exists by missions as a fire exists by burning."[18] The Gospel was consuming the apostle with a holy flame that drove him forward. Jeremiah said, "His word was in my heart as a burning fire shut up in my bones" (Jeremiah 20:9). There was no rest for Paul except for the rest that comes when you know you've done your best for the Lord. Your eyes close in contentment and preparation for what God has for you in the days ahead. The apostle's heart was like a glowing ember fanned to a full blaze by the breath of the Holy Spirit. The fire was spreading. The Gospel was soon to envelop the known world of that day. I am convinced the Apostle Paul was God's greatest tool that facilitated its spread.

As Paul went, he preached; he built churches. He spent those years teaching and discipling others. Discipleship continues throughout our lives as we grow in Christ. Paul knew what James knew: "If any of you lack wisdom, let him ask of God, that giveth to all men liberally, and upbraideth not; and it shall be given him" (James 1:5). Paul's great intellect, zeal, and experience was producing the wisdom of God in all that he said and did. The Holy Spirit guided him into all truth (John 16:13). The Holy Spirit filled Paul with His presence. The mind of Christ had totally captured the mind of Paul. Paul was now ready for missionary ministry of the highest order. He was ready to be the instrument in the hands of the Spirit to write the bulk of the New Testament. He had been "raised up to sit in the heavenly places in Christ Jesus" (Ephesians 2:6). Paul was filled with the Holy Spirit (Ephesians 5:18) perhaps as no other mortal man has ever been. I have seen many people filled with the Spirit, but it is always a temporary thing. Paul's filling seemed to be on a more permanent basis. Those of us who observed the ministry of Dr. Billy Graham were blessed to see a man filled with the Spirit, a life lived in and by the Spirit. However, I believe Dr. Graham would agree that the Apostle Paul rose to much higher and loftier places in his walk than even the great evangelist. Dr. Graham preached the Word; Paul wrote it.

---

18   Brunner, Emil, *The Word and the World*, London: Student Christian Movement Press, 1931, 11

In my visions of the great apostle, I have seen him in relationship to the books that he wrote. I do not feel compelled to try to exegete each book. I walked through the impressive library of Southwestern Baptist Theological Seminary in Fort Worth. I paid particular attention to the rows and rows of books that exegete the writings of the great apostle. It occurred to me that we really don't need another author trying to give us more insight into what Paul wrote. My contribution to the library will be a book that depicts the man and what drove him to write what he wrote.

Having said these things, I do believe that I might lend some insight to the bookends of the books in the New Testament that are most generally attributed to Paul. I believe that Hebrews should actually be first rather than Romans. I believe that Hebrews is a compilation of the sermons that Paul and Apollos preached to the Jews and to the new Christians struggling to maintain their faith. Further, I believe that Dr. Luke may have been the compiler. As I have read the long and varied list of scholars, they attribute the book to Paul, Apollos, Barnabas, Dr. Luke and several others. The arguments in each case offer solutions to some problems but often create others. It is obvious that Paul did not write all of the book. At one point, the writer says that he was not one who saw the risen Lord personally (Hebrews 2:3). Yet, as we read the book, we are struck with so much that is "Pauline." Compare Hebrews 1:3 to Colossians 1:15–17. Compare Hebrews 2:4 to 1 Corinthians 12:11. Compare Hebrews 2:14–17 to Philippians 2:7–8. Compare Hebrews 8:6 to 2 Corinthians 3:6. Other similar comparisons could be made. How then can we explain the various style differences, or the fact that the book does not begin or end as a "normal" letter from the Apostle Paul.

My vision of it all is simplistic. Paul knew Apollos quite well (1 Corinthians 16:12). Their ministries had a certain degree of overlap, as stated in 1 Corinthians 1:6: "I have planted, Apollos watered; but God gave the increase." I believe that they preached in the Jewish synagogues and in the infant churches of the day. The Holy Spirit led them both to preach the superiority of Christ and the superiority of the new covenant. As they shared with one another what they had been given by the Holy Spirit, Dr. Luke was careful to write the messages in a somewhat comprehensive form. The book of Hebrews is perhaps the most powerful answer ever written to the Jewish world. Any Jew of that day would have listened with great interest to the arguments presented.

Many authors have offered outlines for Hebrews, but here's what makes sense to me.

I. The superiority of Christ (Hebrews 1:1–8:6)
II. The superiority of the New Covenant (Hebrews 8:7–10:18)
III. The demands of these superiorities (Hebrews 10:19–13:25)

Each man, Paul and Apollos, had his own way of expressing these powerful truths. As many who believe that Dr. Luke wrote the book point out, the overall grammar of the book is much like that in Luke and Acts. Also, as many point out who support Apollos's authorship of this book, the grammar rises to the level of a classically trained orator. For those who support the idea that Paul was the writer, there is an apostolic ring to that which is said. I must confess that I have always believed that the New Testament is a compilation of books written by men at the direction of the Holy Spirit *and* that these men were *apostles*.

In the desert of Arabia, the Gospel burned in the heart and soul of the Apostle Paul. On weekends, he preached throughout the area. He contended for the faith with the powerful arguments found in the book of Hebrews. As the years passed, the great apostle adapted the message more towards the Greeks and other barbarians. To the Jew, everyone other than Jews were considered barbarians. The New Testament is replete with his letters to churches hewn out of the Greek world. The message does not change from that which he preached to the Hebrew world, but its expression is adapted so that the non-Jew would get the same idea. There is no salvation in any name, other than the name of Jesus.

Now I want to look at the book of Romans. I believe that much of what we read in this great book was given to Paul during his sojourn in the desert of Arabia. Paul's theology was completely reworked. The Old Testament took on a whole new meaning. Law became the springboard for grace. Paul's personal pilgrimage was enveloped in this process. Yet I think it safe to say that the book of Romans is the work of a lifetime of his walk with the Lord. At the end of his ministry, he wrote under the leadership of the Holy Spirit and distilled a lifetime of illumination into this most important of books. I am an old man. I can look back upon how God has led me along, how my faith has been tested, and my understandings have been sharpened.

8

LAST THINGS

I believe that the apostle wanted to go to Spain, as he wanted to go to all the world. However, in the economy of God, he was not allowed to do so. My only proof for this belief is that we have nothing in the New Testament of such a journey. It was said Daniel Boone always wanted to see over the next hill or mountain. Paul wanted to go to Spain.

I believe it would be totally truthful to say that his greatest ambition was to see Jesus. The years in the desert had whetted the apostle's appetite for the closeness of conversation with his Lord. No man *ever* walked with Jesus like Paul. Paul's mind became the mind of Christ. I join Paul in looking forward to that time in heaven's glory that "we shall know even as we are known," that we will have renewed minds on a constant permanent basis, being transformed in every way to living the perfect will of our Lord. With the apostle, I long to be clothed with that new body in the presence of our Great Shepherd of the Sheep, Jesus the Christ, to the Glory of God the Father.

EPILOGUE

Can you see him? Can you see the apostle? Can you see the little man: bald, hooked nose, snarling, angry, a truly *little* man, caught up in his own legalistic ego? Can you see the change that begins on the road to Damascus and gets its greatest push during those three lost years in the Arabian Desert? Can you see the spiritual giant who emerges from the caterpillar of the past to stand taller than Goliath in spiritual terms, clad in the armor of God? This is the general of Jesus taking on the forces of evil throughout the known world, whipping Satan by the power of the Holy Spirit while enduring beatings, stonings, and hardships of all kinds. See the man of faith, whose every thought was Jesus. I see a man who gave himself as a living sacrifice until there was nothing of this world left. His treasure was laid up; his crown was waiting. He lived for Christ but was ready and willing to die for the gain that would be his. When I see him, I see Jesus living his life through Paul. Thank you, Paul, for your devotion to our Savior. Thank you, Jesus, for your servant, Paul. Thank you for using him to explain your great Gospel, that a boy from Notrees, Texas might be saved.

BIBLIOGRAPHY

Barclay, William. *The Gospel of John*, Vol. 2. Philadelphia, PA: The Westminster Press, 1955.

Bombeck, Erma. *If Life Is a Bowl of Cherries, What Am I Doing in the Pits?* Greenwich, CT: Fawcett, 1985.

Brock, W. jun. "Ananias of Damascus." Biblehub. Accessed February, 2023. www.biblehub.com/sermons/auth/brock/ananias_of_damascus.htm.

Bruce, F. F. *Paul: Apostle of the Heart Set Free*. Grand Rapids, MI: Wm. B. Eerdmans Publishing Co., 1977.

Brunner, Emil, *The Word and the World*, London: Student Christian Movement Press, 1931.

Burk, Denny. "Was the Apostle Paul Married?", *Denny Burke: A commentary on theology, politics, and culture*, www.dennyburk.com/wastheapostle-paul-married-yes-he-was-heres-how-we-know/ March 4, 2018

Gaither Vocal Band. "It Is Finished." *Reunited*. Spring House, 2009.

Gladiator. Directed by Ridley Scott. Universal City, CA: Universal Pictures, 2000, network television.

Haynes, Dana. "The Rich Young Ruler is Paul!" *A Faith That Obeys* (blog). July 10, 2020. https://www.afaiththatobeys.org/blog/the-rich-young-ruler-is-paul/.

Hobbs, Herschel H., *The Baptist Faith and Message,* Convention Press, Nashville, TN, 1963

Jackson, Wayne. "Paul's Mother", *Christian Courier,* www.christiancourier.com/articles/pauls-mother, Accessed February 2022

Kennedy, Dr. D.J. *Evangelism Explosion*, Tyndale House Publishers, Wheaton, Illinois, 1970

Kosloski, Philip. "Do You Know Which Book in the Bible is Called "Paul's Gospel"?" *Aleteia*, www.aleteia.org/2019/10/18/do-you-know-which-book-in-the-bible-is-called-pauls-gospel/, 2019

MacArthur, John. "Romans: The Man and the Message", *Grace to You*, www.gty.org/library/sermons-library/45-01/romans-the-man-and-the-message, March 1, 1981

MacArthur, John. "The Armor of God: The Shoes of the Gospel of Peace and the Shield of Faith", Grace to You, www.gty.org/library/sermons-library/90-366/the-armor-of-god-the-shoes-of-the-gospel-of-peace-and-the-shield-of-faith, November 16, 2008

Polhill, John B. *Paul and His Letters*, Nashville, TN: B&H Academic, 1999

Robertson, A.T. *Harmony of the Gospels*, New York, Evanston, and London: Harper & Row, Publishers, 1922

Star Wars: A New Hope, Directed by George Lucas, 20th Century Fox, 1977

The Holy Bible, New International Version, Grand Rapids, MI: Zondervan, 1973. Acts 21:39

Thrillobyte. "Paul Was in Jerusalem during Jesus's Ministry and Crucifixion." City-Data Forum. Posted October 31, 2014. www.city-data.com/forum/christianity/2232303-paul-jerusalem-during-jesus-ministry-crucifixion.

Tomlin, Chris. "Amazing Grace (My Chains Are Gone)", *See the Morning*, Ed Cash, 2006

Warren, Rick. *The Purpose Driven Life*, Zondervan, Grand Rapids, Michigan, 2002

Printed in the United States
by Baker & Taylor Publisher Services